HOW TO BE A CONSERVATIVE

How to be a Conservative

Roger Scruton

BLOOMSBURY CONTINUUM
LONDON · OXFORD · NEW YORK · NEW DELHI · SYDNEY

BLOOMSBURY CONTINUUM
Bloomsbury Publishing Plc
50 Bedford Square, London, WC1B 3DP, UK

BLOOMSBURY, BLOOMSBURY CONTINUUM and the
Diana logo are trademarks of Bloomsbury Publishing Plc

First published 2014
Paperback edition, 2015
New edition, 2019

A catalogue record for this book is available from the British Library

Library of Congress Cataloguing-in-Publication data has been applied for

ISBN: PB: 9781472965233; ePDF: 9781472903785; ePUB: 9781472903778

2 4 6 8 10 9 7 5 3 1

Typeset by Newgen Knowledge Works Pvt. Ltd., Chennai, India
Printed and bound by CPI Group (UK) Ltd, Croydon CR0 4YY

Contents

Preface

The conservative temperament is an acknowledged feature of human societies everywhere. But it is largely in English-speaking countries that political parties and movements call themselves conservative. This curious fact reminds us of the enormous and unacknowledged divide that exists between those places that have inherited the traditions of English common-law government, and those that have not. Britain and America entered the modern world acutely conscious of their shared history. Later, through the traumas of the twentieth century, the two countries stayed together in defence of the civilization that united them, and even today, when Britain, to the general discontent of its people, has joined the European Union, the Atlantic Alliance retains its hold on popular affection, as a sign that we stand for something greater than our creature comforts. Just what is that thing? In the time of Thatcher and Reagan the answer was given in one word: freedom. But that word demands a context. Whose freedom, how exercised, how circumscribed and how defined?

A book has been written in America devoted to the medieval writ of *Habeas corpus* – a writ sent in the king's name commanding whoever might be holding one of his subjects to release that person or to bring him to trial before the king's courts. The continuing validity of this writ, the author argues, underpins American freedom, by making government the servant and not the master of the citizen.[1] Nowhere outside the anglosphere is there the equivalent of *Habeas corpus*, and all attempts to curtail its extent or effect are greeted by English-speaking people with defiance. It expresses, in the simplest possible terms, the unique relation between the government and the governed that has grown from the English common law. That relation is one part of what conservatives uphold in freedom's name.

---

[1] Anthony Gregory, *The Power of Habeas Corpus in America* (Cambridge: Cambridge University Press, 2013).

In explaining and defending conservatism, therefore, I am addressing my remarks primarily to the English-speaking world. I am assuming a readership for whom common-law justice, parliamentary democracy, private charity, public spirit and the 'little platoons' of volunteers describe the default position of civil society, and who have yet to become entirely accustomed to the top-down authority of the modern welfare state, still less to the transnational bureaucracies that are striving to absorb it.

There are two kinds of conservatism, one metaphysical, the other empirical. The first resides in the belief in sacred things and the desire to defend them against desecration. This belief has been exemplified at every point in history and will always be a powerful influence in human affairs. In the concluding chapters of this book I therefore return to it. But for most of the preceding pages I shall be concerned with more down-to-earth matters. In its empirical manifestation, conservatism is a more specifically modern phenomenon, a reaction to the vast changes unleashed by the Reformation and the Enlightenment.

The conservatism I shall be defending tells us that we have collectively inherited good things that we must strive to keep. In the situation in which we, the inheritors both of Western civilization and of the English-speaking part of it, find ourselves, we are well aware of what those good things are. The opportunity to live our lives as we will; the security of impartial law, through which our grievances are answered and our hurts restored; the protection of our environment as a shared asset, which cannot be seized or destroyed at the whim of powerful interests; the open and enquiring culture that has shaped our schools and universities; the democratic procedures that enable us to elect our representatives and to pass our own laws – these and many other things are familiar to us and taken for granted. All are under threat. And conservatism is the rational response to that threat. Maybe it is a response that requires more understanding than the ordinary person is prepared to devote to it. But conservatism is the only response that answers to the emerging realities, and in this book I try to say, as succinctly as I can, why it would be irrational to adopt any other.

Conservatism starts from a sentiment that all mature people can readily share: the sentiment that good things are easily destroyed, but not easily created. This is especially true of the good things that come to us as collective assets: peace, freedom, law, civility, public spirit, the security of property and family life, in all of which we depend on the cooperation of others while having no means singlehandedly to obtain it. In respect of such things, the work of destruction is quick, easy and exhilarating; the work of creation slow, laborious and dull. That is one of the lessons of the twentieth century. It is also one reason why conservatives suffer such a disadvantage when it comes to public opinion. Their position is true but boring, that of their opponents exciting but false.

Because of this rhetorical disadvantage, conservatives often present their case in the language of mourning. Lamentations can sweep everything before them, like the Lamentations of Jeremiah, in just the way that the literature of revolution sweeps away the world of our frail achievements. And mourning is sometimes necessary; without 'the work of mourning', as Freud described it, the heart cannot move on from the thing that is lost to the thing that will replace it. Nevertheless, the case for conservatism does not have to be presented in elegiac accents.[2] It is not about what we have lost, but about what we have retained, and how to hold on to it. Such is the case that I present in this book. I therefore end on a more personal note, with a valediction forbidding mourning.

I have greatly benefited from critical comments made by Bob Grant, Alicja Gescinska and Sam Hughes. It would not have been possible to get my thoughts on to the page without the inspiration, scepticism and occasional satire provided by my wife Sophie, and I dedicate the result to her and our children.

Malmesbury, January 2014

---

[2]   For those interested in the elegiac aspect of my position, see *England: an Elegy* (London: Pimlico, 2001).

My Journey

It is not unusual to be a conservative. But it is unusual to be an intellectual conservative. In both Britain and America some 70 per cent of academics identify themselves as 'on the left', while the surrounding culture is increasingly hostile to traditional values, or to any claim that might be made for the high achievements of Western civilization.[1] Ordinary conservatives – and many, possibly most, people fall into this category – are constantly told that their ideas and sentiments are reactionary, prejudiced, sexist or racist. Just by being the thing they are they offend against the new norms of inclusiveness and non-discrimination. Their honest attempts to live by their lights, raising families, enjoying communities, worshipping their gods, and adopting a settled and affirmative culture – these attempts are scorned and ridiculed by the *Guardian* class. In intellectual circles conservatives therefore move quietly and discreetly, catching each other's eyes across the room like the homosexuals in Proust, whom that great writer compared to Homer's gods, known only to each other as they move in disguise around the world of mortals.

We, the supposed excluders, are therefore under pressure to hide what we are, for fear of being excluded. I have resisted that pressure, and as a result my life has been far more interesting than I ever intended it to be.

I was born towards the end of the Second World War and raised in a lower middle-class household. My father was a trade unionist and a member of the Labour Party, who always wondered whether he had, in becoming a teacher in a primary school, betrayed his working-class origins. For politics, in Jack Scruton's eyes, was the pursuit of class war by other means. Thanks to the unions and the Labour Party, he believed, the working class had begun to drive

---

[1]   See Scott Jaschik, 'Moving Further to the Left', on the website of insidehighered. com (accessed 24 October 2012).

the upper classes into the corner from where they would be forced to deliver up their stolen assets. The major obstacle to this cherished outcome was the Conservative Party, which was an establishment of big business, property developers and landed aristocrats who were hoping to sell the inheritance of the British people to the highest bidder and then move to the Bahamas. Jack regarded himself as locked in a lifelong struggle with this establishment, on behalf of the Anglo-Saxon peasantry whose birthright had been stolen a thousand years earlier by the Norman knights.

It was a story that he found confirmed in our school histories, in the socialist tracts of William Morris and H. J. Massingham, and in his own experience of childhood in the slums of Manchester, from which he had escaped to one of the remaining bits of Old England in the vicinity of the River Thames. There, thanks to a crash course in teacher training, he was able to settle down with my mother, whom he had met when they were both serving with RAF Bomber Command during the war. And his love of Old England grew in him side by side with his resentment at the aristocrats who had stolen it. He believed in socialism, not as an economic doctrine, but as a restoration to the common people of the land that was theirs.

It was difficult living with such a man, especially after I had entered the local grammar school and was on my way to Cambridge, there to be recruited by the class enemy. Nevertheless, I understood from my father just how deeply class feeling had been inscribed in the experience of his generation, and in the northern industrial communities from which he came. I also learned from a very early age that this deep experience had been embellished with a gallery of exciting fictions. The class war, for my father, was the true national epic, sounding in the background to his life as the Trojan War sounds in the background of Greek literature. I did not understand the economic theories of socialism, which I studied in George Bernard Shaw's *Intelligent Woman's Guide to Socialism and Capitalism*. But I knew already that the theories were of little real importance. The fictions were far more persuasive than the facts, and more persuasive than both was the longing to be caught up in a mass movement of solidarity, with the promise of emancipation at the end. My father's grievances were real and well founded. But his solutions were dreams.

There was another side to my father's character, however, and this too greatly influenced me. Robert Conquest once announced three laws of politics, the first of which says that everyone is right-wing in the matters he knows about.[2] My father perfectly illustrated this law. He knew about the countryside, about local history, about the old ways of living, working and building. He studied the villages around High Wycombe, where we lived, and the history and architecture of the town. And through knowing about these matters, he became, in respect of them, an ardent conservative. Here were good things that he wished to conserve. He urged others to join in his campaign to protect High Wycombe and its villages from destruction, threatened as they were by the unscrupulous tactics of developers and motorway fanatics. He founded the High Wycombe Society, gathered signatures for petitions, and gradually raised the consciousness of our town to the point where it made a serious and lasting effort to conserve itself. I shared his love of the countryside and of the old ways of building; I believed, as he did, that the modernist styles of architecture that were desecrating our town were also destroying its social fabric; and I saw, for the first time in my life, that it is always right to conserve things, when worse things are proposed in their place. That *a priori* law of practical reason is also the truth in conservatism.

At the heart of my father's socialism, therefore, lay a deep conservative instinct. And in time I came to understand that the class war that defined his approach to politics was less important to him than the love concealed beneath it. My father deeply loved his country – not the 'UK' of official documents but the England of his walks and reflections. Like the rest of his generation he had seen England in danger and had been called to her defence. He had been inspired by A. G. Street's farming programmes on the BBC Home Service, by Paul Nash's evocative paintings of the English landscape, by H. J. Massingham's writings in *The Countryman*, and by the poetry of John Clare. He had a deep love of English liberty: he believed that the freedom to say what you think and live as you will is something that we English have defended over centuries, and something that would always unite us against tyrants. *Habeas corpus* was inscribed in his heart. He fully bore out the picture of the English working class that had been painted by George Orwell in *The Lion and the Unicorn*. When the chips are down, Orwell argued, our workers do not defend their class but their country, and they associate their country with a gentle way of life in which unusual and eccentric habits – such as not killing one another – are accepted

---

[2] The other two laws are: any organization not explicitly right-wing becomes left-wing in the end; and the simplest way to explain the behaviour of any bureaucratic organization is to assume that it is controlled by a cabal of its enemies.

as the way things are. In these respects, Orwell also thought, the leftist intellectuals will always misunderstand the workers, who want nothing to do with a self-vaunting disloyalty that only intellectuals can afford.

But I too was an intellectual, or fast becoming one. At school and university I rebelled against authority. Institutions, I believed, were there to be subverted, and no codes or norms should be allowed to impede the work of the imagination. But like my father I was also an instance of Conquest's law. The thing I most cared about and which I was determined to make my own was culture – and I included philosophy, as well as art, literature and music under this label. And about culture I was 'right-wing': that is to say, respectful of order and discipline, acknowledging the need for judgement, and wishing to conserve the great tradition of the masters and to work for its survival. This cultural conservatism came to me from the literary critic F. R. Leavis, from T. S. Eliot, whose *Four Quartets* and literary essays entered all our hearts at school, and from classical music. I was deeply struck by Schoenberg's claim that his atonal experiments were not designed to replace the great tradition of German music but to prolong it. The tonal language had lapsed into cliché and kitsch, and it was necessary therefore to 'purify the dialect of the tribe', as Eliot (borrowing from Mallarmé) had expressed the point in *Four Quartets*. This idea, that we must be modern in defence of the past, and creative in defence of tradition had a profound effect on me, and in due course shaped my political leanings.

Leaving Cambridge, and spending a year as *lecteur* in a French *collège universitaire*, I fell in love with France as Eliot once had done. And this led to the decisive change in the focus of my thinking, from culture to politics. May 1968 led me to understand what I value in the customs, institutions and culture of Europe. Being in Paris at the time, I read the attacks on 'bourgeois' civilization with a growing sense that if there is anything half decent in the way of life so freely available in the world's greatest city, the word 'bourgeois' is the proper name for it. The *soixante-huitards* were inheritors of this bourgeois way of life, and enjoyed the freedom, security and wide culture that the French state dispensed to all its citizens. They had every reason to appreciate what France had become under the leadership of General de Gaulle, who had made the French Communist Party as ridiculous in the eyes of the people as it ought also to have been in the eyes of the intellectuals.

To my astonishment, however, the *soixante-huitards* were busy recycling the old Marxist promise of a radical freedom, which will come when private property and the 'bourgeois' rule of law are both abolished. The imperfect freedom that property and law make possible, and on which the *soixante-huitards* depended for their comforts and their excitements, was not enough. That real but relative freedom must be destroyed for the sake of its illusory but absolute shadow. The new 'theories' that poured from the pens of Parisian intellectuals in their battle against the 'structures' of bourgeois society were not theories at all, but bundles of paradox, designed to reassure the student revolutionaries that, since law, order, science and truth are merely masks for bourgeois domination, it no longer matters what you think so long as you are on the side of the workers in their 'struggle'. The genocides inspired by that struggle earned no mention in the writings of Althusser, Deleuze, Foucault and Lacan, even though one such genocide was beginning at that very moment in Cambodia, led by Pol Pot, a Paris-educated member of the French Communist Party.

It is true that only someone raised in the anglosphere could believe, as I believed in the aftermath of 1968, that the political alternative to revolutionary socialism is conservatism. But when I found myself teaching in London University I discovered that my colleagues were standing to a man against something that they described with that very word. Conservatism, they told me, is the enemy, not just of the intellectuals, but also of everyone working for a fair share of the social product, and of everyone 'struggling for peace' against American imperialism. My colleagues were sympathetic to the Soviet Union, whose difficulties, caused by 'capitalist encirclement', had still not been overcome, despite the necessary liquidation of counter-revolutionary elements. But there was an alternative to the revolutionary socialism of Lenin, they believed, which would cure the defects of the Soviet model, and that was the Marxist humanism of the *New Left Review*.

Birkbeck College, where I taught, had begun in the early nineteenth century as the Mechanics Institute, and still upheld its founder George Birkbeck's wish to offer evening classes to people in full-time employment. I therefore had free time during the day, which I devoted to reading for the Bar, thinking that it was only a matter of time before I should need another career. Birkbeck was a secure bastion of the left establishment. Its presiding guru was the communist Eric Hobsbawm, whose histories of the Industrial Revolution remain standard fare in our schools. Its ethos was that of the 'long march through the institutions', which meant rebuilding Britain on the socialist model.

Reading for the Bar, and studying the English law as it was before the pollution injected by the European Courts and before the constitutional changes haphazardly introduced by Tony Blair, I was granted a completely different vision of our society. Common-law justice spoke to me of a community built from below, through the guarantee offered by the courts to all who came before them with clean hands. This vision stayed with me thereafter as a narrative of home. In the English law there are valid statutes and leading cases that date from the thirteenth century, and progressive people would regard this as an absurdity. For me, it was proof that the English law is the property of the English people, not the weapon of their rulers. That thought is not one that you will find in the history books of Hobsbawm.

The political realities of the day had little enough relation to the settled community evoked by Lord Denning in his leading cases, or so clearly observable in our land law and our law of trusts. I vividly recall the surprise I felt, on learning that, under the law of corporations, businesses are obliged to make a profit. How was it that profit, in the 'Ingsoc' of the 1970s, was even allowed, let alone required? At the time the entire management of the country seemed to be devoted to maintaining the steady pace of cultural and economic decline, in the hope of reaching the new and equal society in which everybody would have the same, since nobody would have anything.

Indeed, for many people of conservative temperament, it looked in the late 1970s as though Britain were ready to surrender all that it stood for: its pride, its enterprise, its ideals of freedom and citizenship, even its borders and its national defence. This was the time of CND, the Campaign for Nuclear Disarmament, and the Soviet 'peace offensive', which aimed to disarm the Western Alliance through the work of 'useful idiots', as Lenin had famously described them. The country seemed to be wallowing in feelings of collective guilt, reinforced by a growing culture of dependency. For politicians on the left, 'patriotism' had become a dirty word. For politicians on the right, nothing seemed to matter, save the rush to be a part of the new Europe, whose markets would protect us from the worst effects of post-war stagnation. The *national* interest had been displaced by *vested* interests: by the unions, the establishments and the 'captains of industry'.

The situation was especially discouraging for conservatives. Edward Heath, their nominal leader, believed that to govern is to surrender: we were to surrender the economy to the managers, the education system to the socialists and sovereignty to Europe. The old guard of the Tory Party largely agreed with him, and had joined in the scapegoating of Enoch Powell, the only one among them who had publicly dissented from the post-war consensus. In the bleak years of the 1970s, when a culture of repudiation spread through the universities and the opinion-forming elites, it seemed that there was no way back to the great country that had successfully defended our civilization in two world wars.

Then, in the midst of our discouragement, Margaret Thatcher appeared, as though by a miracle, at the head of the Conservative Party. I well remember the joy that spread through the University of London. At last there was someone to hate! After all those dreary years of socialist consensus, poking in the drab corners of British society for the dingy fascists who were the best that could be found by way of an enemy, a real demon had come on the scene: a leader of the Tory Party, no less, who had the effrontery to declare her commitment to the market economy, private enterprise, the freedom of the individual, national sovereignty and the rule of law – in short to all the things that Marx had dismissed as 'bourgeois ideology'. And the surprise was that she did not mind being hated by the left, that she gave as good as she got, and was able to carry the people with her.

I never swallowed in its entirety the free-market rhetoric of the Thatcherites. But I deeply sympathized with Thatcher's motives. She wanted the electorate to recognize that the individual's life is his own and the responsibility of living it cannot be borne by anyone else, still less by the state. She hoped to release the talent and enterprise that, notwithstanding decades of egalitarian claptrap, she believed yet to exist in British society. The situation she inherited was typified by the National Economic Development Council, set up under a lame Conservative government in 1962, in order to manage the country's economic decline. Staffed by big-wigs from industry and the civil service, 'Neddy', as it was known, devoted itself to perpetuating the illusion that the country was in 'safe hands', that there was a plan, that managers, politicians and union leaders were in it together and working for the common good. It epitomized the post-war British establishment, which addressed the nation's problems by appointing committees of the people who had caused them.

Neddy's ruling idea was that economic life consists in the management of existing industries, rather than the creation of new ones. Wilson, Heath and Callaghan had all relied upon Neddy to confirm their shared belief that, if you held on long enough, things would come out OK and any blame would fall on your successor. By contrast, Margaret Thatcher believed that, in business as in politics, the buck stops here. The important person in a free economy is not the manager but the entrepreneur – the one who takes risks and meets the cost of them. Whether Thatcher succeeded in replacing an economy of management and vested interests with one of entrepreneurship and risk may of course be doubted. By liberating the labour market she put the economy on an upward climb. But the long-term result has been the emergence of a new managerial class, as the multinationals move in with their takeover bids, their legal privileges and their transnational lobbyists for whom small businesses and entrepreneurs are the enemy. Those who object to this new managerialism (and I am one of them) should nevertheless recognize that what is bad in it is precisely what was bad in the old corporatist economy that Thatcher set out to destroy. When she claimed that entrepreneurs create things, while managers entomb them, it was immediately apparent that she was right, since the effects of the management culture lay all around us.

I say it was immediately apparent, but it was not apparent to the intellectual class, which has remained largely wedded to the post-war consensus to this day. The idea of the state as a benign father-figure, who guides the collective assets of society to the place where they are needed, and who is always there to rescue us from poverty, ill health or unemployment, has remained in the foreground of academic political science in Britain. On the day of Margaret Thatcher's death I was preparing a lecture in political philosophy at the University of St Andrews. I was interested to discover that the prescribed text identified something called the New Right, associated by the author with Thatcher and Reagan, as a radical assault on the vulnerable members of society. The author assumed that the main task of government is to distribute the collective wealth of society among its members, and that, in the matter of distribution, the government is uniquely competent. The fact that wealth can be distributed only if it is first created seemed to have escaped his notice.

Of course Thatcher was not an intellectual, and was motivated more by instinct than by a properly worked out philosophy. Pressed for arguments, she leaned too readily on market economics, and ignored the deeper roots of conservatism in the theory and practice of civil society. Her passing remark that 'there is no such thing as society' was gleefully seized upon by my university colleagues as proof of her crass individualism, her ignorance of social philosophy, and her allegiance to the values of the new generation of businessmen, which could be summarized in three words: money, money, money.

Actually what Thatcher meant on that occasion was quite true, though the opposite of what she said. She meant that there *is* such a thing as society, but that society is not identical with the state. Society is composed of people, freely associating and forming communities of interest that socialists have no right to control and no authority to outlaw. To express it in that way, however, was not

Thatcher's style and not what her followers expected of her. What the British public wanted, and what they got, was the kind of instinctive politician whom they could see at once to be speaking for the nation, whether or not she had the right fund of abstract arguments.

Understandably, she felt the winds of intellectual scorn that blew around her, and sheltered behind a praetorian guard of economic advisers versed in 'market solutions', 'supply-side economics', 'consumer sovereignty', and the rest. But those fashionable slogans did not capture her core beliefs. All her most important speeches as well as her enduring policies stemmed from a consciousness of national loyalty. She believed in our country and its institutions, and saw them as the embodiment of social affections nurtured and stored over centuries. Family, civil association, the Christian religion and the common law were all integrated into her ideal of freedom under law. The pity was that she had no philosophy with which to articulate that ideal, so that 'Thatcherism' came to denote a kind of caricature of conservative thinking, created by the left in order to cover the right with ridicule.

Not that Thatcher was without influence on her leftist critics. She so changed things that it became impossible for the Labour Party to wrap itself again in its Victorian cobwebs: Clause IV (the commitment to a socialist economy) was dropped from its constitution, and a new middle-class party emerged, retaining nothing of the old agenda apart from the desire to punish the upper class, and the belief that the way to do this is by banning fox-hunting, to which cause 220 hours of Parliamentary time were devoted under the administration of Tony Blair (who allowed just 18 hours of discussion before going to war in Iraq).

At the time, however, it was not Thatcher's impact on domestic policy that was most vividly felt but her presence on the international stage. Her commitment to the Atlantic alliance, and preparedness to stand side by side with President Reagan in defiance of the Soviet threat, entirely changed the atmosphere in Eastern Europe. Quite suddenly people who had been broken and subdued by the totalitarian routine learned that there were Western leaders who were prepared to press for their liberation. John O'Sullivan has forcefully argued that the simultaneous presence in the highest offices of Reagan, Thatcher and Pope John Paul II was the cause of the Soviet collapse.[3] And my own experience confirms this.

[3] See John O'Sullivan, *The President, the Pope and the Prime Minister: Three Who Changed the World* (Washington, DC: Regnery, 2006).

For it was about this time that I underwent a new political awakening. During the 1970s, I had worked with a group of friends to set up the Conservative Philosophy Group, with the intention of bringing Parliamentarians, conservative journalists and academics together to discuss the foundations of their shared worldview. And then in 1979, I wrote *The Meaning of Conservatism* – an impetuous attempt to counter the free market ideology of the Thatcherite think tanks. I wanted to remind conservatives that there *is* such a thing as society, and that society is what conservatism is all about. I believed that 'freedom' is not a clear or sufficient answer to the question of what conservatives believe in. Like Matthew Arnold, I held that 'freedom is a very good horse to ride, but to ride *somewhere*'.

I had not troubled myself to imagine, during those years of Thatcher's rise, what would happen to our still secure and comfortable world, were all basic freedoms to be taken away. I was cocooned in the false security of an introspective island, with no knowledge of the realm of fear and negation that the communists had installed just a little way to the east of us. A visit to Poland and Czechoslovakia in 1979 awoke me to the reality. I encountered first-hand the thing that Orwell perceived when fighting alongside the communists in the Spanish Civil War and which he expressed in telling images in *Nineteen Eighty-Four*. I saw the translation into fact of the fictions that swam in the brains of my Marxist colleagues. I entered Hobsbawmia, and felt the malign enchantment of a wholly disenchanted world.

I had been asked to give a talk to a private seminar in Prague. This seminar was organized by Julius Tomin, a Prague philosopher who had taken advantage of the Helsinki Accords of 1975, which supposedly obliged the Czechoslovak government to uphold freedom of information and the basic rights defined by the UN Charter. The Helsinki Accords were a farce, used by the communists to identify potential troublemakers, while presenting a face of civilized government to gullible intellectuals in the West. Nevertheless, I was told that Dr Tomin's seminar met on a regular basis, that I would be welcome to attend it, and that they were indeed expecting me.

I arrived at the house, after walking through those silent and deserted streets, in which the few who stood seemed occupied on some dark official business, and in which party slogans and symbols disfigured every building. The staircase of the apartment building was also deserted. Everywhere the same expectant silence hung in the air, as when an air raid has been announced, and the town hides from its imminent destruction. Outside the apartment, however, I encountered two policemen, who seized me as I rang the bell and demanded my papers. Dr Tomin came out, and an altercation ensued, during which I was pushed down the stairs. But the argument continued and I was able to push my way up again, past the guards and into the apartment. I found a room full of people, and the same expectant silence. I realized that there really was going to be an air raid, and that the air raid was me.

In that room was a battered remnant of Prague's intelligentsia – old professors in their shabby waistcoats; long-haired poets; fresh-faced students who had been denied admission to university for their parents' political 'crimes'; priests and religious in plain clothes; novelists and theologians; a would-be rabbi; and even a psychoanalyst. And in all of them I saw the same marks of suffering, tempered by hope; and the same eager desire for the sign that someone cared enough to help them. They all belonged, I discovered, to the same profession: that of stoker. Some stoked boilers in hospitals; others in apartment blocks; one stoked at a railway station, another in a school. Some stoked where there were no boilers to stoke, and these imaginary boilers came to be, for me, a fitting symbol of the communist economy.

This was my first encounter with 'dissidents': the people who, to my later astonishment, would be the first democratically elected leaders of post-communist Czechoslovakia. And I felt towards these people an immediate affinity. Nothing was of such importance for them as the survival of their national culture. Deprived of material and professional advancement, their days were filled with a forced meditation on their country and its past, and on the great Question of Czech History that has preoccupied the Czechs since the movement for national revival in the nineteenth century. They were forbidden to publish; the authorities had concealed their existence from the world, and had resolved to remove their traces from the book of history. Hence the dissidents were acutely conscious of the value of memory. Their lives were an exercise in what Plato called *anamnesis*: the bringing to consciousness of forgotten things. Something in me responded immediately to this poignant ambition, and I was at once eager to join with them and make their situation known to the world. And I recognized that *anamnesis* described the meaning of my life too.

Thus began a long connection with the unofficial networks in Poland, Czechoslovakia and Hungary, through which I learned to see socialism in another way – not as a dream of idealists, but as a real system of government, imposed from above and maintained by force. I awoke to the fraud that had been committed in socialism's name, and felt an immediate obligation to do something about it. All those laws formulated by the British Labour Party, which set out to organize society for the greater good of everyone, by controlling, marginalizing or forbidding some natural human activity, took on another meaning for me. I was suddenly struck by the impertinence of a political party that sets out to confiscate whole industries from those who had created them, to abolish the grammar schools to which I owed my education, to force schools to amalgamate, to control relations in the workplace, to regulate hours of work, to compel workers to join a union, to ban hunting, to take property from a landlord and bestow it on his tenant, to compel businesses to sell themselves to the government at a dictated price, to police all our activities through quangos designed to check us for political correctness. And I saw that this desire to control society in the name of equality expresses exactly the contempt for human freedom that I encountered in Eastern Europe. There is indeed such a thing as society; but it is composed of individuals. And individuals must be free, which means being free from the insolent claims of those who wish to redesign them.

My adventures in the communist world coincided with another adventure at home – the establishment of a journal of conservative thought, the *Salisbury Review*, named after the great prime minister whose greatness consists in the fact that nobody knows anything about him, even though he held office for close on 20 years. The *Review* was run on a shoestring, and for a while I had great difficulty in persuading the few conservatives of my acquaintance to write for it. My original intention was to stimulate intellectual debate concerning the concepts of modern political thought, so as to move conservatism away from free-market economics. But things took an explosive turn when Ray Honeyford, headmaster of a school in Bradford, sent me an article advocating the integration of the new minorities through the educational system, and lamenting the isolationism of the Pakistani families whose children he was striving to teach. I published the article and immediately the thought police got wind of it.

Ray Honeyford was an upright, conscientious teacher, who believed it to be his duty to prepare children for responsible life in society, and who was confronted with the question of how to do this, when the children are the offspring of Muslim peasants from Pakistan, and the society is that of England. Honeyford's article honestly conveyed the problem, together with his proposed solution, which was to integrate the children into the surrounding secular culture, while protecting them from the punishments administered in their pre-school classes in the local *madrasah*, meanwhile opposing their parents' plans to take them away whenever it suited them to Pakistan. He saw no sense in the doctrine of multiculturalism, and believed that the future of our country depends upon our ability to integrate its recently arrived minorities, through a shared curriculum in the schools and a secular rule of law that could protect women and girls from the kind of abuse to which he was a distressed witness.

Everything Ray Honeyford said is now the official doctrine of our major political parties: too late, of course, to achieve the results that he hoped for, but nevertheless not too late to point out that those who persecuted him and who surrounded his school with their inane chants of 'Ray-cist' have never suffered, as he suffered, for their part in the conflict. Notwithstanding his frequently exasperated tone, Ray Honeyford was a profoundly gentle man, who was prepared to pay the price of truthfulness at a time of lies. But he was forcibly retired, and the teaching profession lost one of its most humane and public-spirited representatives. This was one example of a prolonged Stalinist purge by the educational establishment, designed to remove all signs of patriotism from our schools and to erase the memory of England from the cultural record. Henceforth the *Salisbury Review* was branded as a 'racist' publication, and my own academic career thrown into doubt.

The conflicts in which I became involved over the ensuing years, brought home to me just how low the level of public debate had sunk in Britain. On the left there seemed to be no response to the enormous changes introduced by mass immigration except to describe everyone who attempted to discuss the matter as a 'racist'. This crime resembled the crime of being an *émigré* in Revolutionary France, or a bourgeois in Lenin's Russia: the accusation was proof of guilt. And yet nobody ever told us what the crime consisted in. I was reminded of Defoe's comment, at the time of the Popery Act of 1698, that 'the streets of London are full of stout fellows prepared to fight to the death against Popery, without knowing whether it be a man or a horse'.

I was the more astonished to discover that this elementary intellectual defect had entirely invaded the political science departments of our universities, and that the intellectual world was in a fever about the presence among us of 'racists' whose conspiracy could never be discovered and whose nature could never be clearly defined. Being classed as a racist gave me a faint intimation of what it has been like, in other times, to belong to some despised and persecuted minority. After a particularly frightening episode in which I was chased from a public lecture in the University of York, and following libels by the BBC and *The Observer* I decided to leave the academic world and live by my wits.

By this time – 1989 – the Berlin wall had fallen, and I was able to return to Czechoslovakia, where I had been arrested and expelled in 1985. Together with friends and colleagues, I set up a government relations business that bumped along for a few years, providing me with a small income. Observing the volatile nature of the new democracies, I came vividly to see how unimportant a part of democracy are elections, in comparison with the enduring institutions and public spirit that make elected politicians accountable. The rule in Eastern Europe, following the collapse of communism, was for a group of adventurers to form a political party, to win an election on the strength of grandiose promises, and then to privatize as much as possible to themselves before being wiped out at the next election. To my amazement, the European Union nevertheless decided to extend its reach into these new democracies. The market-based legal order of the Brussels bureaucracy helped to fill the legal vacuum created by communism, and was warmly received on that account. But, because of the unwise provisions of the Treaty of Rome regarding freedom of movement, it has led to the mass emigration of the professional classes, and to the loss of the educated young from countries that stand desperately in need of them. The 'enlargement' agenda has therefore become controversial all across Europe, and I return to the controversy in what follows.

Those experiences helped to convince me that European civilization depends upon the maintenance of national borders, and that the EU, which is a conspiracy to dissolve those borders, has become a threat to European democracy. Through the operation of the European courts and the shape of its legislation, the EU has created a political class which is no longer accountable to the people – a class typified by Baroness Ashton, a former CND *apparatchik* who has never stood for an election in her life and who has advanced through Labour Party quangos and leftist NGOs to become Commissioner in charge of Foreign Relations, in other words, the foreign minister of our continent. The European Commission itself passes laws that cannot be overridden by national parliaments, following discussion behind closed doors among bureaucrats who need never answer for their decisions.

The comic attempt to draw up a constitution for Europe produced a document so long and involved as to be all but unintelligible. The preamble managed to exclude the Christian religion from the idea of Europe, while the rest of the document – which was far more about extending the powers of the European institutions than setting limits to them – was calculated to kill off democracy. Given that Europe's legacy to the world consists in the two great goods of Christianity and democracy it is hardly surprising if the EU no longer has the endorsement of the European people, even if it has created a network of clients upon whose support it can always rely.

At a certain point in the 1980s I found myself in Lebanon, visiting the communities that were striving to survive in the face of Hafiz al-Assad's brutal attempt to create a Greater Syria. My experiences there awoke me to two vital truths about the world in which we live. The first is that you do not create boundaries by drawing lines on the map, as the French and British had done at the end of the First World War. Boundaries arise through the emergence of national identities, which in turn require that religious obedience take second place to the feeling for home, territory and settlement. Moreover, as the example of Lebanon in so many ways illustrates, democracy will always be jeopardized in places where identities are confessional rather than territorial.

The second truth impressed on me was that, for the very reason that Islam puts religion above nationality as the test of membership, Islamism poses a threat to political order. This is particularly true of the Islamism of the Muslim Brotherhood and its erstwhile leader Sayyid Qutb, for whom, in the contest between the *shari'ah* and the modern world, it is the modern world that must go. In response to the Lebanese tragedy I wrote a short book – *A Land Held Hostage* – in which I pleaded for the old Lebanese order. I defended the Lebanese constitution, which had been designed to foster a shared national identity that would stand above the confessional identities that divide village from village and neighbour from neighbour all across the land that they share. And I warned against the ambitions of Hezbollah, the 'Party of God', which was attempting to establish a regional Shi'ite power network, under the aegis of Syria and Iran.

The conflict between Sunni and Shi'a has now come to dominate the region, and my futile plea on behalf of the old Lebanon counted for nothing. But this experience taught me that our civilization cannot survive if we continue to appease the Islamists. I later argued the point in *The West and the Rest*, a book published in 2002, in response to the atrocities of 9/11; in writing it I came to see that, precious though national boundaries are, yet more precious is the civilization that has made national boundaries perceivable.

That civilization is rooted in Christianity, and it is by seeing our world in Christian terms that I have been able to accept the vast changes that have shaken it. Acceptance comes from sacrifice: that is the message conveyed by so many of the memorable works of our culture. And in the Christian tradition the primary acts of sacrifice are confession and forgiveness. Those who confess, sacrifice their pride, while those who forgive, sacrifice their resentment, renouncing thereby something that had been dear to their hearts. Confession and forgiveness are the habits that made our civilization possible.

Forgiveness can be offered only on certain conditions, and a culture of forgiveness is one that implants those conditions in the individual soul. You can forgive those who have injured you only if they acknowledge their fault. This acknowledgement is not achieved by saying 'yes, that's true, that's what I did'. It requires penitence and atonement. Through these self-abasing acts, the wrongdoer goes out to his victim and re-establishes the moral equality that makes forgiveness possible. In the Judaeo-Christian tradition all this is well known, and incorporated into the sacraments of the Roman Catholic Church as well as the rituals and liturgy of Yom Kippur. We have inherited from those religious sources the culture that enables us to confess to our faults, to make recompense to our victims, and to hold each other to account in all matters where our free conduct can harm those who have cause to rely on us.

Accountability in public office is but one manifestation of this cultural inheritance, and we should not be surprised that it is the first thing to disappear when the utopians and the planners take over. Nor should we be surprised that it is absent from the world of the Islamists – even though forgiveness has an important place in the practice of Islam and in the morality of the Koran.[4] What we are now seeing in the wake of the 'Arab Spring' is the inside of governments in which accountability had no place – governments in which power was the only commodity. And the experience reminds us of an important truth, which is that accountable government does not come through elections. It comes through respect for law, through public spirit and through a culture of confession. To think that there is a merely accidental connection between those virtues and our Judaeo-Christian heritage is to live in cloud cuckoo land. It is to overlook the culture that has focused, down the centuries, on the business of repentance. Understanding this in my own life has made me see it all the more clearly in the context of politics. It is precisely this aspect of the human condition that was denied by the totalitarian systems of the twentieth century.

---

[4]   See, for example, Koran, 13, 22. This is not to say that the message of the Koran is identical in this respect with that contained in the Judaeo-Christian tradition. Both Jesus and Rabbi Hillel placed love and forgiveness at the centre of morality; for the Koran that central place is occupied by submission. Love and forgiveness may be *signs* of submission; but they are not what it essentially is.

And the desire to deny it underlies the anti-Christian turn of the European Union and the sly dictatorship of its elites.

Having said that, I acknowledge that the conservative philosophy that I summarize in what follows in no way depends on the Christian faith. The relation between them is subtler and more personal than that implies. The argument of this book is addressed to the reader, regardless of his or her religious convictions, since it is about living in the empirical world, not believing in the transcendental. Whatever our religion and our private convictions, we are the collective inheritors of things both excellent and rare, and political life, for us, ought to have one overriding goal, which is to hold fast to those things, in order to pass them on to our children.

2

Starting from Home

We live in great societies, and depend in a thousand ways on the actions and desires of strangers. We are bound to those strangers by citizenship, by law, by nationality and neighbourhood. But those bonds between us do not, in themselves, suffice to solve the great problem that we share, which is the problem of coordination. How is it that we can pursue our lives in relative harmony, each enjoying a sphere of freedom and all pursuing goals of our own? In *The Wealth of Nations*, Adam Smith argued that self-interest can solve this problem. Given a free economy and an impartial rule of law, self-interest leads towards an optimal distribution of resources. Smith did not regard economic freedom as the sum of politics, nor did he believe that self-interest is the only, or even the most important, motive governing our economic behaviour. A market can deliver a rational allocation of goods and services only where there is trust between its participants, and trust exists only where people take responsibility for their actions and make themselves accountable to those with whom they deal. In other words, economic order depends on moral order.

In *The Theory of the Moral Sentiments*, Smith emphasized that trust, responsibility and accountability exist only in a society that respects them, and only where the spontaneous fruit of human sympathy is allowed to ripen. It is where sympathy, duty and virtue achieve their proper place that self-interest leads, by an invisible hand, to a result that benefits everyone. And this means that people can best satisfy their interests only in a context where they are also on occasion moved to renounce them. Beneath every society where self-interest pays off, lies a foundation of self-sacrifice.

We are not built on the model of *homo oeconomicus* – the rational chooser who acts always to maximize his own utility, at whatever cost to the rest of us. We are subject to motives that we do not necessarily understand, and which can be displayed in terms of utilities and preference orderings only by misrepresenting them. These motives make war on our circumstantial desires. Some of them – the fear of the dark, the revulsion towards incest, the impulse to cling to the mother – are adaptations that lie deeper than reason. Others – guilt, shame, the love of beauty, the sense of justice – arise from reason itself, and reflect the web of interpersonal relations and understandings through which we situate ourselves as free subjects, in a community of others like ourselves. At both levels – the instinctive and the personal – the capacity for sacrifice arises, in the one case as a blind attachment, in the other case as a sense of responsibility to others and to the moral way of life.

The error of reducing political order to the operations of the market parallels the error of revolutionary socialism, in reducing politics to a plan. In his *Reflections on the French Revolution*, Edmund Burke argued against the 'geometrical' politics, as he called it, of the French revolutionaries – a politics that proposed a rational goal, and a collective procedure for achieving it, and which mobilized the whole of society behind the resulting programme. Burke saw society as an association of the dead, the living and the unborn. Its binding principle is not contract, but something more akin to love. Society is a shared inheritance for the sake of which we learn to circumscribe our demands, to see our own place in things as part of a continuous chain of giving and receiving, and to recognize that the good things we inherit are not ours to spoil. There is a line of obligation that connects us to those who gave us what we have; and our concern for the future is an extension of that line. We take the future of our community into account not by fictitious cost-benefit calculations, but more concretely, by seeing ourselves as inheriting benefits and passing them on.

Burke's complaint against the revolutionaries was that they assumed the right to spend all trusts and endowments on their own self-made emergency. Schools, church foundations, hospitals – all institutions that had been founded by people, now dead, for the benefit of their successors – were expropriated or destroyed, the result being the total waste of accumulated savings, leading to massive inflation, the collapse of education and the loss of the traditional forms of social and medical relief. In this way, contempt for the dead leads to the disenfranchisement of the unborn, and although that result is not, perhaps, inevitable, it has been repeated by all subsequent revolutions. Through their contempt for the intentions and emotions of those who had laid things by, revolutions have systematically destroyed the stock of social capital, and always revolutionaries justify this by impeccable utilitarian reasoning. *Homo oeconomicus* enters the world without social capital of his own, and he consumes whatever he finds.

Society, Burke believed, depends upon relations of affection and loyalty, and these can be built only from below, through face-to-face interaction. It is in the family, in local clubs and societies, in school, workplace, church, team, regiment and university that people learn to interact as free beings, taking responsibility for their actions and accounting to their neighbours. When society is organized from above, either by the top-down government of a revolutionary dictatorship, or by the impersonal edicts of an inscrutable bureaucracy, then accountability rapidly disappears from the political order, and from society too. Top-down government breeds irresponsible individuals, and the confiscation of civil society by the state leads to a widespread refusal among the citizens to act for themselves.

In place of top-down government, Burke made the case for a society shaped from below, by traditions that have grown from our natural need to associate. The important social traditions are not just arbitrary customs, which might or might not have survived into the modern world. They are forms of knowledge. They contain the residues of many trials and errors, as people attempt to adjust their conduct to the conduct of others. To put it in the language of game theory, they are the discovered solutions to problems of coordination, emerging over time. They exist because they provide necessary information, without which a society may not be able to reproduce itself. Destroy them heedlessly and you remove the guarantee offered by one generation to the next.

In discussing tradition, we are not discussing arbitrary rules and conventions. We are discussing *answers* that have been discovered to enduring *questions*. These answers are tacit, shared, embodied in social practices and inarticulate expectations. Those who adopt them are not necessarily able to explain them, still less to justify them. Hence Burke described them as 'prejudices', and defended them on the ground that, though the stock of reason in each individual is small, there is an accumulation of reason in society that we question and reject at our peril. Reason shows itself in that about which we do not, and maybe cannot, reason – and this is what we see in our traditions, including those that contain sacrifice at the heart of them, such as military honour, family attachment, the forms and curricula of education, the institutions of charity and the rules of good manners.

Tradition is not theoretical knowledge, concerning facts and truths; and not ordinary know-how either. There is another kind of knowledge, which involves the mastery of situations – knowing *what to do*, in order to accomplish a task successfully, where success is not measured in any exact or pre-envisaged goal, but in the harmony of the result with our human needs and interests. Knowing what to do in company, what to say, what to feel – these are things we acquire by immersion in society. They cannot be taught by spelling them out but only by osmosis; yet the person who has not acquired these things is rightly described as ignorant. The divisions of the day, the assignment of tasks in a family, the routines of a school, a team or a court, the liturgy of a church, the weights and measures used in everyday business, the clothes that are chosen for this or that social need: all these embody tacit social knowledge without which our societies would crumble. There are examples nearer to the heart of politics too: the British Crown, incorporating a myriad subtle roles and offices; the common law, evolving from the steady flow of precedents; parliamentary and congressional procedures, with their prerogatives and formalities.

Political philosophers of the Enlightenment, from Hobbes and Locke, reaching down to John Rawls and his followers today, have found the roots of political order and the motive of political obligation in a social contract – an agreement, overt or implied, to be bound by principles to which all reasonable citizens can assent. Although the social contract exists in many forms, its ruling principle was announced by Hobbes with the assertion that there can be 'no obligation on any man which ariseth not from some act of his own'.[1] My obligations are my own creation, binding because freely chosen. When you and I exchange promises, the resulting contract is freely undertaken, and any breach does violence not merely to the other but also to the self, since it is a repudiation of a well-grounded rational choice. If we could construe our obligation to the state on the model of a contract, therefore, we would have justified it in terms that all rational beings must accept. Contracts are the paradigms of self-chosen obligations – obligations that are not imposed, commanded or coerced but freely undertaken. When law is founded in a social contract, therefore, obedience to the law is simply the other side of free choice. Freedom and obedience are one and the same.

Such a contract is addressed to the abstract and universal *Homo oeconomicus* who comes into the world without attachments, without, as Rawls puts it, a 'conception of the good', and with nothing save his rational self-interest to guide him. But human societies are by their nature exclusive, establishing privileges and benefits that are offered only to the insider, and which cannot be freely bestowed on all-comers without sacrificing the trust on which social harmony depends. The social contract begins from a thought-experiment, in which a group of people gather together to decide on their common future.

[1]   Thomas Hobbes, *Leviathan*, Part 2, Chapter 21.

But if they are in a position to decide on their common future, it is because they already have one: because they recognize their mutual togetherness and reciprocal dependence, which makes it incumbent upon them to settle how they might be governed under a common jurisdiction in a common territory. In short, the social contract requires a relation of membership. Theorists of the social contract write as though it presupposes only the first-person singular of free rational choice. In fact, it presupposes a first-person plural, in which the burdens of belonging have already been assumed.

Even in the American case, in which a decision was made to adopt a constitution and make a jurisdiction *ab initio*, it is nevertheless true that a first-person plural was involved in the very making. This is confessed to in the document itself. 'We, the people ...' Which people? Why, *us*; we who *already belong*, whose historic tie is now to be transcribed into law. We can make sense of the social contract only on the assumption of some such pre-contractual 'we'. For who is to be included in the contract? And why? And what do we do with the one who opts out? The obvious answer is that the founders of the new social order already belong together: they have already imagined themselves as a community, through the long process of social interaction that enables people to determine who should participate in their future and who should not.

Furthermore, the social contract makes sense only if future generations are included in it. The purpose is to establish an enduring society. At once, therefore, there arises that web of non-contractual obligations that links parents to children and children to parents and that ensures, willy-nilly, that within a generation the society will be encumbered by non-voting members, dead and unborn, who will rely on something other than a mere contract between the living if their rights are to be respected and their love deserved. Even when there arises, as in America, an idea of 'elective nationality', so that newcomers may choose to belong, *what* is chosen is precisely not a contract but a bond of membership, whose obligations and privileges transcend anything that could be contained in a defeasible agreement.

There cannot be a society without this experience of membership. For it is this that enables me to regard the interests and needs of strangers as my concern; that enables me to recognize the authority of decisions and laws that I must obey, even though they are not directly in my interest; that gives me a criterion to distinguish those who are entitled to the benefit of the sacrifices that my membership calls from me, from those who are interloping. Take away the experience of membership and the ground of the social contract disappears: social obligations become temporary, troubled and defeasible, and the idea that one might be called upon to lay down one's life for a collection of strangers begins to border on the absurd. Moreover, without the experience of membership, the dead will be disenfranchised, and the unborn, of whom the dead are the metaphysical guardians, will be deprived of their inheritance. Unless the 'contract between the living' can be phrased in such a way that the dead and the unborn are a part of it, it becomes a contract to appropriate the earth's resources for the benefit of its temporary residents. Philosophers of the social contract, such as John Rawls, are aware of this problem;[2] but to my mind they have failed to discover the motives that would lead ordinary people to sign up to a contract that spreads their obligations into the distant future. Critics of Western societies do not hesitate to point out that the squandering of resources is exactly what has happened, since the contractual vision of society gained ground over the experience of membership that made it possible.[3]

We can envisage society as founded in a contract only if we see its members as capable of the free and responsible choice that a contract requires. But only in certain circumstances will human beings develop into rational choosers, capable of undertaking obligations and honouring promises, and oriented towards one another in a posture of responsibility. In the course of acquiring this posture towards others, people acquire obligations of quite another kind – obligations to parents, to family, to place and community, upon all of which they have depended for the nurture without which the human animal cannot develop into the human person. Those obligations are not obligations of justice, such as arise from the free dealings of human adults. The Romans knew them as obligations of piety (*pietas*), meaning that they stem from the natural gratitude towards what is *given*, a gratitude that we spontaneously direct to the gods. Today we are reluctant to provide these obligations with such a theological backing, though it is important to see that, for religious believers, unchosen obligations are not only vital to the building from below of a durable social order, but also properly owed to God.

Human beings, in their settled condition, are animated by *oikophilia*: the love of the *oikos*, which means not only the home but the people contained in

2   See the discussion of the 'just savings principle' in *A Theory of Justice* (Oxford: Harvard University Press, 1971), section 44.
3   See in this connection the account of the 'market state' developed by Philip Bobbitt, in *The Shield of Achilles: War, Peace and the Course of History* (New York: Alfred A. Knopf, 2002).

it, and the surrounding settlements that endow that home with lasting contours and an enduring smile.[4] The *oikos* is the place that is not just mine and yours but *ours*. It is the stage-set for the first-person plural of politics, the locus, both real and imagined, where 'it all takes place'. Virtues like thrift and self-sacrifice, the habit of offering and receiving respect, the sense of responsibility – all those aspects of the human condition that shape us as stewards and guardians of our common inheritance – arise through our growth as persons, by creating islands of value in the sea of price. To acquire these virtues we must circumscribe the 'instrumental reasoning' that governs the life of *Homo oeconomicus*. We must vest our love and desire in things to which we assign an intrinsic, rather than an instrumental, value, so that the pursuit of means can come to rest, for us, in a place of ends. That is what we mean by settlement: putting the *oikos* back in the *oikonomia*. And that is what conservatism is about.[5]

People settle by acquiring a first-person plural – a place, a community and a way of life that is 'ours'. The need for this 'we' is not accepted by internationalists, by revolutionary socialists, or by intellectuals wedded to the Enlightenment's timeless, placeless vision of the ideal community. But it is a fact, and indeed the primary fact from which all community and all politics begin. George Orwell noticed this, during the course of the Second World War. The disloyalty of the left intelligentsia was, for Orwell, all the more evident and all the more shocking, when set beside the simple, dogged 'we' of the ordinary people. And the real political choice, about which Orwell had no hesitation, was whether to join the intellectuals in their work of destruction, or to stand by the ordinary people in defending their country in its hour of need.

There are two ways in which the first-person plural can emerge: it can emerge through a shared purpose, or it can emerge through a shared lack of purpose. Purposeless things are not necessarily useless things, nor are all useless things worthless. Consider friendship. Friends are valued for their own sake; and the benefits of friendship are not what we value, but by-products of the thing that we value, obtainable only by the person who does not pursue them. In the scope of human life, purposeless things like friendship are supremely useful: they are ends, not means, the places of fulfilment and homecoming, the goal of every pilgrimage. Without them, our purposes are null and void.

---

[4] I have developed this point in *Green Philosophy: How to Think Seriously about the Planet* (London: Atlantic Books and New York: Oxford University Press, 2012).
[5] See *Green Philosophy*, op. cit., for the proof of what I say in that paragraph.

The lesson of recent history, for me, is that purposeful arrangements crumble as the purpose fades, while purposeless arrangements endure. We saw this clearly in communist Europe. In all countries under Soviet control, the party was outside the law, without legal personality, and unaccountable to the citizens or to its members. It was shaped by the ruling purpose, which was to create a new society on socialist principles, abolishing everything that stood in the way. All of politics was justified in terms of the future socialist order, towards which society was moving inexorably, the party leading from the front, the secret police whipping behind. No institution was permitted to exist that was not subject to party control, with one exception, the Polish Catholic Church, which had been able to negotiate special terms for itself – a dispensation that proved fatal to the communist experiment when a Polish priest was elected to the papacy. Charities were illegal and there was no way in which private individuals could hold property in trust for a communal use. Society was entirely *instrumentalized*, in pursuit of the one overriding purpose of 'building socialism'. All associations were kept together by the top-down commands of the party, and those commands were justified in terms of a purpose, in which, as it happened, nobody believed. The work of the secret police was to control and if possible prevent free association, so that society would be entirely atomized by suspicion and fear. Each person would be allowed to secure what he or she could in his own private corner, behind the back of the great machine that gave the orders. But all association was to occur under the guidance of the party. The communist citizen was to be the perfect *Homo oeconomicus*, motivated by rational self-interest to advance a purpose that was no one's.

To the dismay of the authorities, however, people formed friendships; they got together to read, to study, to make music. And even if the ever-vigilant secret police from time to time disrupted their meetings, the fact is that through these meetings the life of society renewed itself, in little platoons that were insulated from the all-obliterating commands of the socialist state. People discovered, in their personal lives, that civil society is not goal-directed. It comes into being, in whatever circumstances, as an end in itself, a form of life that is appreciated for what it is, not for what it does.

Michael Oakeshott earned a well-deserved reputation as a political thinker through his lifelong attempt to understand the nature of 'civil association', as he called it – the kind of association in which our political aspirations find equilibrium and completion. In *On Human Conduct*, he based his theory of political order on a contrast between civil association and 'enterprise association'.[6] In enterprise, people combine for a purpose, and their association is predicated on the need to cooperate in order to achieve it. Enterprise associations are of many kinds: for example, there is the army, in which top-down commands, relayed through the ranks of subordinates, point always to the single end of defeating the enemy; there is business, in which purposes may fluctuate from day to day, though with the overriding need for profit in the long run; there are the various forms of learning that train people for the professions and the trades.

Oakeshott believed that civil association has been increasingly displaced by enterprise, under pressure from political elites, managers, parties and ideologues. It is not only socialists with their goals of equality and social justice who have contributed to this displacement. The liberal attempt to adopt the contours of an abstract and universal idea of justice and human rights; the supposedly conservative pursuit of economic growth as the root of social order and the goal of government – these too have a tendency to displace civil association with a new kind of political practice, in which the institutions of society are bent towards a goal that may be incompatible with their inner dynamic.

The distinction between civil and enterprise association is not hard and fast: many of our social spheres partake of both arrangements. Nevertheless, it is hard to deny that enterprise tends in a different direction from ordinary forms of community. In enterprise there are instructions coming down from above; there are rivalries and rebellions; there is ruinous failure as well as temporary success. The whole depends on a forward-going energy that must be constantly maintained if things are not to fragment and fall apart. Hence the invocations of 'progress', of 'growth', of constant 'advance' towards the goal which, however, must remain always somewhere in the future, lest the dedication of the citizens cease to be renewed by it.

In *Die Welt von Gestern*, Stefan Zweig attributed the decline of civil order in Europe to the myth of progress.[7] In all the ideologies of his day – communism, socialism, Nazism, fascism – Zweig saw the same pernicious attempt to rewrite the principles of social order in terms of a linear progression from past to future. The cult of the leader, of the 'vanguard party', of the 'avant-garde' – all supposed that society has a *direction*, in the way that businesses have a purpose

---

[6] Michael Oakeshott, *On Human Conduct* (London: Oxford University Press, 1975).
[7] Stefan Zweig, *Die Welt von Gestern* (Stockholm: Bermann-Fischer, 1942); *The World of Yesterday* (New York: Viking, 1943).

and armies have a goal. And all licensed the increasing conscription of the citizen, and the steady absorption of the functions of society into the machinery of the state.

The most important political effect of this displacement of civil by enterprise association has been the gradual loss of authority and decision-making from the bottom of society, and its transfer to the top. If you supply society with a dynamic purpose, especially one conceived in these linear terms, as moving always forwards towards greater equality, greater justice, greater prosperity or, in the case of the EU, 'ever closer union', you at the same time license the would-be leaders. You give credentials to those who promise to guide society along its allotted path, and you confer on them the authority to conscript, dictate, organize and punish the rest of us, regardless of how we might otherwise wish to lead our lives. In particular, you authorize the invasion of those institutions and associations that form the heart of civil society, in order to impose on them a direction and a goal that may have nothing to do with their intrinsic nature.

This happened to the institutions of education in Britain and America, when the egalitarians targeted them in the 1960s. It became government policy to view schools not as associations for the transmission of knowledge, with their own internal purposes that develop according to the needs and desires of their members, but as instruments of social engineering. Curriculum, examinations, admissions and discipline were all to be revised in the light of their contribution to the ruling purpose, which was the elimination of distinctions and unfair advantages, so that all children would enter society with an equal chance of a worthwhile life.

Egalitarians believed that there could be a mutually beneficial trade-off between social and educational purposes: such is the assumption behind the vast literature of educational reform that was propagated through the schools of education in the 1960s. Schools, it was argued, are not devoted uniquely to passing exams; they are places where children associate, and where their future prospects are influenced in a thousand ways. Why should we not adapt the curriculum and the timetable in ways that equalize their chances?

To argue in that way is to ignore the distinction between the internal purpose of an institution and its incidental effects. Those who join in a game of football are intent on scoring goals: if they neglect that purpose, then the game ceases to exist. But the incidental effects of their participation are many: exercise, companionship, delight. Good though those effects are they cannot be made into the purpose of the game, without destroying the game, so losing the good effects of it. In just such a way, the many good effects of education arise not because they are pursued but because they are *not* pursued: they arise as the by-product of pursuing something else, which is knowledge. If knowledge is seen merely as a means to confer social advantages, and not pursued for its own sake, then both knowledge and the advantages conferred by it will be lost. When pursued for its own sake, however, knowledge ceases to be common property. Its advantages will always be unequally distributed. We should not be surprised, therefore, at the educational decline that we have witnessed throughout the Western world since the egalitarian agenda was imposed on the schools. It is the inevitable result of confiscating the real goal of education, which is education, conceived as an end in itself, and replacing it with another that no school can coherently aim at or reliably supply, which is equality.

To what extent is settlement available now? How, in a world of fungible relationships, ubiquitous commercialization, rapid migration and constant erosion of our social and political inheritance can conservatives draw the line at the things that should not be changed? Can there be a settlement in which everyone and everything is in motion, and if so, can conservatives raise their standard in such a place, and say that just this is the order we defend? Even if we accept the argument that I have given for pre-political membership, even if we acknowledge that membership must be conceived in Oakeshott's terms, as civil association freed from some overarching purpose, we must acknowledge that, without a measure of stability, it is unlikely that such an arrangement will produce the trust on which civil society and political order both depend.

The second law of thermodynamics tells us that entropy is always increasing, and that every system, every organism, every spontaneous order will, in the long term, be randomized. Is not the conservative simply someone who cannot accept this truth – the truth, as the Anglo-Saxon poem puts it, that 'this too will pass'? In response I say that the transience of human goods does not make conservatism futile, any more than medicine is futile, simply because 'in the long run we are all dead', as Keynes famously put it. Rather, we should recognize the wisdom of Lord Salisbury's terse summary of his philosophy and accept that 'delay is life'.

Conservatism is the philosophy of attachment. We are attached to the things we love, and wish to protect them against decay. But we know that they cannot last forever. Meanwhile we must study the ways in which we can retain them through all the changes that they must necessarily undergo, so that our lives are still lived in a spirit of goodwill and gratitude. The argument that follows will attempt to outline exactly what remains to us, why it is valuable, how we can keep it, and with it the freedom and satisfaction that we, the beneficiaries of Western civilization, have learned to take for granted.

3

The Truth in Nationalism

When the French Revolutionaries burst onto the stage of world politics it was with the declaration that henceforth it is not the sovereign, or the law, or the deity that will command the allegiance of the citizen, but the nation. The Abbé Sieyès, in his inflammatory pamphlet, *What is the Third Estate?* of 1789, expressed the point succinctly. 'The nation is prior to everything. It is the source of everything. Its will is always legal … The manner in which a nation exercises its will does not matter; the point is that it does exercise it; any procedure is adequate, and its will is always the supreme law.' Twenty years and two million deaths later, when the will of the French nation had been spread across Europe by Napoleon's conquests, it was clear that a wholly new conception of political life had entered the consciousness of Europe. All across the continent, nationalist movements were calling people to arms against local monarchs and imperial settlements, rallying them in the name of fictitious ideas of race and kinship, championing one language against another and one way of life against its neighbour, and in general unsettling whatever remained to be unsettled after the mess that Napoleon had made.

The resulting devastation has been described by Adam Zamoyski, in *Holy Madness*, and has been the subject of endless commentary from historians searching for the causes of the two world wars.[1] By the time that peace was established after 1945, with Germany in ruins and the nation states of Eastern Europe firmly under Soviet control, a kind of consensus was emerging among the new political class – the class that was tasked with the reconstruction of the defeated nations. According to this consensus, Europe had been torn apart by nationalism, and the future of the continent could be guaranteed only if the national loyalties that had caused so much belligerence were quietly and

---

[1]   Adam Zamoyski, *Holy Madness: Romantics, Patriots and Revolutionaries* (London: Weidenfeld, 2001).

discreetly replaced by something else. Just what that something else was to be is another question, and the question was buried so deeply in the process of European integration that it is no longer possible to answer it.

But was the reaction against nationalism right? To put my answer in a nutshell: nationalism, as an ideology, is dangerous in just the way that ideologies are dangerous. It occupies the space vacated by religion, and in doing so excites the true believer both to worship the national idea and to seek in it for what it cannot provide – the ultimate purpose of life, the way to redemption and the consolation for all our woes. That is the national idea as Sieyès invokes it, and as it appears in the literature of Nazi Germany. But it is not the idea of the nation as this features in the ordinary day-to-day life of the European people. For ordinary people, living in free association with their neighbours, the 'nation' means simply the historical identity and continuing allegiance that unites them in the body politic. It is the first-person plural of settlement. Sentiments of national identity may be inflamed by war, civil agitation and ideology, and this inflammation admits of many degrees. But in their normal form these sentiments are not just peaceful in themselves, but a form of peace between neighbours.

It is because we are able to define our membership in territorial terms that we, in Western countries, enjoy the elementary freedoms that are, for us, the foundation of political order. In states founded on religious, rather than secular, obedience, freedom of conscience is a scarce and threatened asset. We, however, enjoy not merely the freedom publicly to disagree with others about matters of faith and private life, but also the freedom to satirize solemnity and to ridicule nonsense, including solemnity and nonsense of the sacred kind.

By the end of the seventeenth century, as the Enlightenment spread its influence far and wide across the Christian world, it was beginning to be accepted that we manage our affairs in this world by passing our own laws, and that these laws are man-made, secular, and if possible neutral when it comes to the various religions that compete within the state. Should there be an apparent clash between secular law and religious obedience, it has become accepted in our society that secular law prevails. The hope has been that the two spheres of duty, the sacred and the secular, are sufficiently separate, so that there would in any case be little or no overlap between them. To put it bluntly, religion, in our society, has become a private affair, which makes no demands of the public as a whole.

It should not be doubted that our inheritance of secular law is precious, and something that we should hold onto in the face of the many threats to it. It is our principal defence against what Tocqueville and John Stuart Mill denounced as the tyranny of the majority. Majority opinion may be wrong; majority desires may be wicked; majority strength may be dangerous. There is someone more important than the majority, namely the person who disagrees with it. We must protect that person. He is the one who can raise the question that no crowd wants to listen to, which is the question whether it is in the right. Until opposition is protected, therefore, there is no door through which reason can enter the affairs of government. But how is opposition protected? What makes it possible for people to agree to disagree?

In families, people often get together to discuss matters of shared concern. There will be many opinions, conflicting counsels, and even factions. But in a happy family everyone will accept to be bound by the final decision, even if they disagree with it. That is because they have a shared investment in staying together. Something is more important to all of them than their own opinion, and that is the family, the thing whose welfare and future they have come together to discuss. To put it in another way: the family is part of their *identity*; it is the thing that does not change, as their several opinions alter and conflict. A shared identity takes the sting from disagreement. It is what makes opposition, and therefore rational discussion, possible; and it is the foundation of any way of life in which compromise, rather than dictatorship, is the norm.

The same is true in politics. Opposition, disagreement, the free expression of dissent and the rule of compromise all presuppose a shared identity. There has to be a first-person plural, a 'we', if the many individuals are to stay together, accepting each other's opinions and desires, regardless of disagreements. Religion provides such a first-person plural: I might define myself as a Christian or a Muslim, and that might be sufficient to bind me to my fellow believers, even when we disagree on matters of day-to-day government. But that kind of first-person plural does not sit easily with democratic politics. In particular it does not accept the most fundamental disagreement within the state, between the faithful who accept the ruling doctrine and the infidels who don't.

That is why democracies need a national rather than a religious or an ethnic 'we'. The nation state, as we now conceive it, is the by-product of human neighbourliness, shaped by an 'invisible hand' from the countless agreements between people who speak the same language and live side by side. It results from compromises established after many conflicts, and expresses the slowly forming agreement among neighbours both to grant each other space and to protect that space as common territory. It has consciously absorbed and adjusted to the ethnic and religious minorities within its territory, as they in turn have adjusted to the nation state. It depends on localized customs and a shared routine of tolerance. Its law is territorial rather than religious and invokes no source of authority higher than the intangible assets that its people share.

All those features are strengths, since they feed into an adaptable form of pre-political loyalty. Unless and until people identify themselves with the country, its territory and its cultural inheritance – in something like the way people identify themselves with a family – the politics of compromise will not emerge. We have to take our neighbours seriously, as people with an equal claim to protection, for whom we might be required, in moments of crisis, to face mortal danger. We do this because we believe ourselves to *belong together* in a *shared home*. The history of the world is proof of this: wherever people identify themselves in terms that are not shared by their neighbours then the state falls apart at the first serious blow – as has happened in the former Yugoslavia, in Syria, in Somalia and in Nigeria today.

There is another and deeper reason for adhering to the nation as the source of legal obligation. Only when the law derives from national sovereignty can it adapt to the changing conditions of the people. We see this clearly in the futile attempt of modern Islamic states to live by the *shari'ah*. The original schools of Islamic jurisprudence, which arose in the wake of the Prophet's reign in Medina, permitted jurists to adapt the revealed law to the changing needs of society, by a process of reflection known as *ijtihād*, or effort. But this seems to have been brought to an end during the eighth century of our era, when it was maintained by the then dominant theological school that all important matters had been settled and that the 'gate of *ijtihād* is closed'.[2] This seemed to be the only way to conserve the authority of God's absolute and eternal decrees, in the face of human deviousness and backsliding. Hence today, when the clerics take over, law is referred back to precepts designed for the government of a long-since-vanished community. Jurists have great difficulty in adapting such a law to the life of modern people.

To put the point in a nutshell – secular law adapts, religious law endures. Moreover, precisely because the *shari'ah* has not adapted, nobody really knows what it says. Does it tell us to stone adulterers to death? Some say yes, some say

---

[2]   See Robert Reilly, *The Closing of the Muslim Mind* (Wilmington, DE: ISI Books, 2011).

no. Does it tell us that investing money at interest is in every case forbidden? Some say yes, some say no. When God makes the laws, the laws become as mysterious as God is. When *we* make the laws, and make them for our purposes, we can be certain what they mean. The only question then is 'Who are *we*?' And, in modern conditions, the nation is the answer to that question, an answer without which we are all at sea.

As I remarked, in the wake of the Second World War the political elite in the defeated nations became sceptical towards the nation state. The European Union arose from the belief that the European wars had been caused by national sentiment, and that what is needed is a new, trans-national form of government, which will unite people around their shared interest in peaceful coexistence. Unfortunately, people don't identify themselves in that way. There is no first-person plural of which the European institutions are the political expression. The Union is founded in a treaty, and treaties derive their authority from the entities that sign them. Those entities are the nation states of Europe, from which the loyalties of the European people derive. The Union, which has set out to transcend those loyalties, therefore suffers from a permanent crisis of legitimacy.

Laws laid down by God have the changeless and inscrutable character of their author. But the same is true of laws laid down by treaties. Treaties are dead hands, which should be laid upon a country only for specific and essential purposes, and never as a way of governing them. Thus, when the Treaty of Rome was signed in 1957 it included a clause permitting the free movement of capital and labour between the signatories. At the time, incomes and opportunities were roughly similar across the small number of states who signed. Now things are very different. The European Union has expanded (without a popular mandate) to include most of the former communist states of Eastern Europe, whose citizens now have the legal right to take up residence within British national borders, competing for jobs at a time when Britain has over 2 million unemployed, and when its infrastructure and urban fabric are showing the strain of overpopulation. A great many British citizens are unhappy with this. But because the law permitting it is inscribed within the treaty, and because the treaty takes precedence over parliamentary legislation, there is nothing that can be done about it. It is just as though the British, too, were governed by a kind of religious law, in which the will of God sounds through every edict, preventing even the most necessary change for reasons that can never be fathomed.

Why did the experiment in federal government, which has led to an unaccountable empire in Europe, lead to a viable democracy in America? The answer is simple: because American federalism created not an empire but a nation state. This happened despite the dispute over states rights, despite the Civil War, despite the legacy of slavery and ethnic conflict. It happened because the American settlement established a secular rule of law, a territorial jurisdiction and a common language in a place that the people were busily claiming as their *home*. Under the American settlement, people were to treat each other, first and foremost, as *neighbours*: not as fellow members of a race, a class, an ethnic group or a religion, but as fellow settlers in the land that they shared. Their loyalty to the political order grew from the obligations of neighbourliness; and disputes between them were to be settled by the *law of the land*. The law was to operate within territorial boundaries defined by the prior attachments of the people, and not by some trans-national bureaucracy open to capture by people for whom those boundaries meant nothing.

In short, democracy needs boundaries, and boundaries need the nation state. All the ways in which people come to define their identity in terms of the *place where they belong* have a part to play in cementing the sense of nationhood. For example, the common law of the Anglo-Saxons, in which laws emerge from the resolution of local conflicts, rather than being imposed by the sovereign, has had a large part to play in fostering the English and American sense that the law is the common property of all who reside within its jurisdiction rather than the creation of priests, bureaucrats or kings. A shared language and shared curriculum have a similar effect in making familiarity, proximity and day-to-day custom into sources of a shared attachment. The essential thing about nations is that they grow from below, through habits of free association among neighbours, and result in loyalties that are attached to a place and its history, rather than to a religion, a dynasty, or, as in Europe, to a self-perpetuating political class. Nations can amalgamate into more complex wholes – as Wales, Scotland and England have amalgamated – or they can break apart like the Czechs and the Slovaks, or as the United Kingdom will one day break apart as the Scots reclaim their sovereignty. National boundaries can be weak or strong, porous or impregnable: but in all forms they provide the people with an identity with which to summarize their rights and duties as citizens, and their allegiance to those on whom they most nearly depend for civic peace.

Here, then, is the truth in nationalism, as I see it. When we ask ourselves the question, to what do we belong, and what defines our loyalties and commitments, we do not find the answer in a shared religious obedience, still less in bonds of tribe and kinship. We find the answer in the things that we share with our fellow citizens, and in particular in those things that serve to sustain the rule of law and the consensual forms of politics.

First among these things is territory. We believe ourselves to inhabit a shared territory, defined by law, and we believe that territory to be *ours*, the place where we are, and where our children will be in turn. Even if we came here from somewhere else, that does not alter the fact that we are committed to this territory, and define our identity – at least in part – in terms of it.

Of almost equal importance are the history and customs through which that territory has been settled. There are rituals and customs that occur here and which bind neighbours together in a shared sense of home. These rituals and customs may include religious services, but these are by no means essential, and are open to reinterpretation when it is necessary to include some neighbour who does not share our faith. Increasingly, therefore, the stories and customs of the homeland are secular. The stories may not be literally true; they may include large areas of myth, like the stories that the French tell about Jeanne d'Arc, about the Bastille and about the Revolution, or the stories that the Scots tell about Robert the Bruce and about the Jacobite rebellions. The stories are the product of shared loyalty and not the producer of them: the loyalty does not come about because the stories are believed; the stories are believed because the loyalty needs them. And the stories change to accommodate the changing first-person plural of the people. They are, as Plato put it, noble lies: literal false-hoods expressing emotional truths. A rational being will see through them, but nevertheless respect them, as he respects religious convictions that he does not share, and the heroes of other nations.

Hence national myths tend to be of three kinds: tales of glory, tales of sacrifice and tales of emancipation, each reflected in the history books of the day. Victorian histories tell the tale of the Blessed Isle and its defence, of the Glorious Revolution, and the building of the great empire on which the sun never set. From behind those tales of glory emerges a tale of sacrifice, which was the national myth that sustained the British people through the two world wars. Nothing epitomizes this transition from glory to sacrifice more poignantly than the Ealing Studios film *Scott of the Antarctic*, made in 1948 to commemorate the spirit that had seen the British people through the privations of the Second World War. As we would see it now, Scott's expedition had no motive other than the competitiveness of schoolboys; it was the ultimate futile gesture, in which the virtues of the English were put to the supreme test. Scott and his team were the transcendental image of the 'good loser': the player who sacrifices everything with a smile, and who lies buried far from home with no achievement apart from the honourable conduct that led to his end. Victory in the Second World War had cost the British people all that they had. But in the death of Scott was the mystical proof that loss is gain.

The myth of sacrifice has since given way to the myth of emancipation, and the history books rewritten yet again. Now the tale of Britain begins with the emancipation of the slaves, moves through the emancipation of the workers to the suffragettes and the emancipation of women, and finally to the emancipation of everyone in the equal society of today: that is the myth presented in Danny Boyle's opening ceremony for the 2012 London Olympics, and received with pride by the crowds. It defines the new history curriculum in our schools, and although it contains hardly a grain of truth, it has the singular advantage – which it shares with the French stories of the Revolution – that it can be accepted by people on the left and so bind us all in a shared identity.

Our national narrative may change, but what underlies it is something that remains always in place: the secular law. We who have been brought up in the English-speaking world have internalized the idea that law exists to do justice between individual parties, rather than to impose a uniform regime of commands. Other Western systems have also reinforced the attachment of citizens to the political order – notably Roman law and its many derivatives (the *code napoléon* among them). It was evident from the earliest days of Christianity that the New Testament was not an attempt to replace the law of the imperial power, but an attempt to make a space for spiritual growth within it. In his parables, Christ emphasized that the secular law is to be obeyed, and that our duty to God does not require us to defy or to replace it. Nor should we pay too much attention to the finicky edicts of the Torah, since 'the Sabbath was made for man, and not man for the Sabbath'.

To someone raised on the doctrine that legitimate law comes from God, and that obedience is owed to Him above all others, the claims of the secular jurisdiction are regarded as at best an irrelevance, at worst a usurpation. Such is the message of Sayyid Qutb's writings, and of *Milestones (ma'alim fi'l tariq*, 1964) in particular. In that book, Qutb denounces secular law, national identity and the attempt to establish a purely human political order without reference to the revealed will of God: all are blasphemous in Qutb's eyes. Qutb's followers have included Osama Bin Laden and his successor Ayman al-Zawahiri, both of whom wished to establish in the Arabian Peninsula the rule of God, so that the law revealed to the Prophet could govern the Prophet's homeland, as a first stage towards governing everywhere else. Meanwhile their base – *al-qa'eda* – has been established in cyberspace, a fitting location for a cause that is nowhere in particular, and everywhere in general.

What the Islamist movements promise to their adherents is not citizenship under a territorial jurisdiction but *brotherhood* – *ikhwān* – under the reign of God. Although the professed goal is the worldwide Islamic *ummah*, in which all the faithful will be united in a shared obedience, the actual experience of brotherhood is selective and exclusive; it never spreads very far without exposing itself to sudden and violent refutation. The association of brothers is not a new entity, a corporation, which can negotiate for its members. It remains essentially plural – *ikhwān* being the plural of *akh*, brother, and used to denote the assembly of likeminded people brought together by their common commitment, rather than any institution that can claim sovereignty over them or represent them in the eyes of the world. Brothers don't take orders: they act together as a family, until they quarrel and fight.[3]

The distinctions I have been making between the Western political inheritance, based on secular law, citizenship and the nation state, and the traditional Islamic view, based on divine law, brotherhood and submission to a universal faith, are of course only part of the story. In all kinds of ways the Islamic world has been shifting in new directions, and the difference between a country like Iran, with a once dissident Shi'ite faith, and a long history of religious scholarship and humane letters, and a country like Yemen, in parts of which life still resembles that known to the Prophet, is as great as the difference between either and any Western state. Nevertheless, the Islamic world remains suspicious of the national divisions imposed on it by the Western powers and the United Nations. It is therefore inevitable that Islamists should turn their resentment on the West, as the creator and imposer of an alien form of political order.

Opposition to the nation idea does not come only from outside, however. If you look at the organs of opinion in Britain and Europe, and at the institutions, such as universities, in which the self-consciousness of European societies is expressed and developed, you find almost everywhere a culture of *repudiation*.

---

[3] This point connects with the lack of corporate personality in Islamic law. For the consequences of this, see Malise Ruthven, *Islam in the World* (Oxford: Oxford University Press, 1984, 3rd edn 2006).

Take any aspect of the Western inheritance of which our ancestors were proud, and you will find university courses devoted to deconstructing it. Take any positive feature of our political and cultural inheritance, and you will find concerted efforts in both the media and the academy to place it in quotation marks, and make it look like an imposture or a deceit. And there is an important segment of political opinion on the left that seeks to endorse these critiques and to convert them into policies.

It is to this 'culture of repudiation', as I call it, that we should attribute the recent attacks on the nation state and the national idea. But conservatism is a culture of affirmation. It is about the things we value and the things we wish to defend. Anybody who understands what is at stake in the global conflict that is developing today will, I believe, come to see that the nation is one of the things that we must keep. In what follows, therefore, I shall be appealing to people who identify their political rights and duties in national terms, and who have learned to put God in the place where He belongs.

4

The Truth in Socialism

Socialists believe that, in some deep sense, human beings are all equal, and that, when it comes to the advantages conferred by membership of society, this equality ought to show itself in the way people are treated. Quite what equal treatment means is, of course, controversial. Criminals are not treated in the same way as law-abiding citizens; old, frail and crippled people are not treated in the same way as the able-bodied. But socialism means, for most of its advocates, a political programme designed to secure for all citizens an equal *chance* of a fulfilling life, whether or not that chance is finally realized. If people choose to spoil their chances, or to gain an unfair advantage through crime, then they must suffer the consequences. But most socialists today adhere to a doctrine of 'social justice', according to which it is not a misfortune but an *injustice* when upright honest people start life with disadvantages that they cannot rectify by their own efforts, and which present an immovable obstacle to receiving the benefits of social membership.

That idea of social justice may not be coherent. But it speaks to sentiments that we share. I have argued that the political process, as we in Western democracies have inherited it, depends upon citizenship, which in turn depends upon a viable first-person plural. And in the previous chapter I gave what to me are incontrovertible arguments for construing that first-person plural in national terms.

No such first-person plural can emerge in a society divided against itself, in which local antagonisms and class war eclipse every understanding of a shared destiny. Hence British conservatives in the nineteenth century frequently acknowledged common cause with the Chartists, and the greatest conservative thinker of the Victorian age, John Ruskin, addressed many of his homilies to the urban working class. Disraeli was not the inventor of 'One Nation' Toryism, but he certainly made clear, in the preface to *Sybil*, that the conservative cause would be lost if it did not also appeal to the new migrants to the industrial towns, and if it did not take their situation seriously. A believable conservatism has to suggest ways of spreading the benefit of social membership to those who have not succeeded in gaining it for themselves.

It is because we cooperate in societies that we enjoy the security, prosperity and longevity to which we have become accustomed, and which were unknown, even to the minority of aristocrats, before the twentieth century. The way in which our activities are woven together, binding the destiny of each of us to that of strangers whom we shall never know, is so complex that we could never unravel it. The fiction of a social contract fails to do justice to all the relations – promising, loving, coercing, pitying, helping, cooperating, forbidding, employing, dealing – that bind the members of society into an organic whole. Yet the benefit of membership is inestimable. Hobbes may have been wrong to think that he could reduce the obligation of society to a contract; but he was surely right to think that outside society life would be 'solitary, poor, nasty, brutish and short'. And the more we take from this arrangement, the more we must give in return. This is not a contractual obligation. It is an obligation of gratitude. But it exists for all that, and must be built into the conservative vision as a cornerstone of social policy.

That, in my view, is the truth in socialism, the truth of our mutual dependence, and of the need to do what we can to spread the benefits of social membership to those whose own efforts do not suffice to obtain them. *How* this is to be done is an intricate political question. The situation of Europe today, well over a century after Bismarck's invention of the welfare state, provides many object-lessons in how welfare benefits might be extended to the unemployable and the unemployed, and how health care might be offered as a public resource, either free on demand or else as a system of publicly funded compensation for expenditure properly incurred. Every system has attendant disadvantages as well as virtues. But all have proved subject to two defects.

First, they contribute to the creation of a new class of dependants – people who have come to depend on welfare payments, perhaps over several genera-tions, and who have lost all incentive to live in another way. Often the system of benefits is so devised that any attempt to escape from it by working will lead to a loss, rather than a gain, in family income.[1] And once the cycle of reward is established, it creates expectations that are passed on in the families

---

[1]   See the essays in Frank Field, *Welfare Titans, and Other Essays on Welfare Reform* (London: Civitas, 2002), for some examples.

of those who enjoy them. Habits such as out-of-wedlock birth, malingering and hypochondria are rewarded, and the habits are passed on from parent to child, creating a class of citizens who have never lived from their own industry and know no one else who has done so either. The cost of this is not primarily economic: it directly impacts on the sentiment of membership, antagonizing those who live in a responsible way, and separating the dependant minority from the full experience of citizenship.[2]

The other defect is that welfare systems, as so far devised, have an open-ended budget. Their cost is constantly increasing: free health care, which extends the life of the population, leads to ever-increasing health-care costs at the end of life, and also to pension liabilities that cannot be met from existing funds. As a result, governments are increasingly borrowing from the future, mortgaging the assets of the unborn for the benefit of the living. The ever-increasing public debt has until now been serviced, on the assumption that governments don't default and will not default while the level of debt remains at the present order of magnitude. But trust in government debt has been heavily shaken by recent events in Greece and Portugal, and should this trust evaporate, so will the welfare state – at least in its existing form.

The truth in socialism, therefore, points towards a major and growing political problem. Two things prevent modern governments from addressing this problem. The first is that the issue has been politicized, to the extent that the truth is often dangerous to express and certainly difficult to act upon. The second is that the issue lies on the very frontier of debates about the nature of the state. When Marx was at work on *Das Kapital* and the *Communist Manifesto*, it seemed natural to refer to the division of classes in the language of war. In the Marxian vision the proletariat, who own nothing but their labour power, are exploited by the bourgeoisie who, by owning the means of production, are able to extort the hours of 'unpaid labour' that accumulate in their hands as 'surplus value'. For Marx, the relation between bourgeoisie and proletariat was essentially antagonistic, and was forecast to lead to open class war when the 'wage slaves' rise up to dispossess their masters. But this war has broken out only where intellectuals have been able to foment it – as Lenin did in Russia and Mao in China, neither of which countries possessed a real urban working class.

[2] For a detailed analysis of the American case, see Charles Murray, *Losing Ground: American Social Policy, 1950-1980* (New York: Basic Books, 1984).

The wars of the twentieth century brought home the fundamental truth that people will fight for their country and unite in its defence, but will seldom fight for their class, even when the intellectuals are egging them on. At the same time, people expect the state to reward their loyalty. The modern welfare state emerged from the twentieth-century wars therefore as a matter of course, and in response to a consensus. Now that its reform is urgently needed, so too is the consensus that led to its foundation.

As the dispute over 'Obamacare' has shown, that consensus is not available in America. Unlike the Medicare provisions, which were brought in by negotiation between the two principal parties, 'Obamacare' was the initiative of a single party, did not have the consent of the opposition and was concealed within 2,000 pages of legislative jargon that was never properly explained either to the public or to the members of Congress. Not surprisingly, therefore, the legislation has led to a polarization of opinion and a breakdown in the political process, each side claiming to represent the interests of the people, but neither side convinced that 'the people' includes those who did not vote for it.

Likewise, recent attempts by the British Conservative Party to reform the system of benefits, with a view to removing the poverty trap and making the system affordable, have been criticized from the left as an 'attack on the poor and the vulnerable'. All across the Western world the welfare state is becoming unaffordable in its present form, and the constant borrowing from the future will only make its collapse more devastating when it comes. Yet seldom will a governing party risk embarking on radical reform, for fear of giving a hostage to the left, for whom this is not just an iconic issue, but a way of summoning its captive voters.

The debates have been distorted by the widespread adoption of a relative definition of poverty. Peter Townsend, in *Poverty in the United Kingdom*, published in 1979,[3] defined poverty as 'relative deprivation', meaning the comparative inability to enjoy the fruits of surrounding affluence. He concluded that 15 million Britons (a quarter of the total) lived on or near the margins of poverty. In a similar spirit, the last Labour government defined poverty as the condition of someone who receives less than 60 per cent of the median income. Since it is inevitable, given the unequal distribution of human talent, energy and application, that there will be people with less than 60 per cent of the median

---

[3]   Peter Townsend, *Poverty in the United Kingdom* (Harmondsworth: Penguin Books 1979).

income this definition implies that poverty will never go away, regardless of how wealthy the poorest are. By this sleight of hand it has been possible to berate governments on behalf of the poor, however much their policies raise the standard of living. The relative definition serves also to perpetuate the great socialist illusion, which is that the poor are poor because the rich are rich. The implication is that poverty is cured only by equality, and never by wealth.

The other great obstacle to coherent thinking about poverty is the central role now occupied by the state in the lives of its clients. When your budget is provided by the state then you will vote for the politician who promises to augment it. In this way it has proved possible for parties of the left to build up reliable block votes, paying for these votes with the taxes of those who vote the other way. This involvement of the state in the most basic decisions of its dependants radically curtails the room for manoeuvre. In France today a dwindling body of middle-class taxpayers is asked to maintain so many state dependants that the top rate of tax has to be raised to 75 per cent in order to meet the budget – and even then does not meet it, since rates of tax at that level lead to the emigration or voluntary idleness of those capable of paying them.

I have referred to the truth in socialism. But this truth has been packaged with falsehoods. One of these falsehoods is the doctrine that the welfare state manages the social product as a common asset, 'redistributing' wealth, so as to ensure that all have the share to which they are entitled. This picture, according to which the products of human labour are essentially unowned until the state distributes them, is not merely the default position of left-wing thought. It has been programmed into academic political philosophy, so as to become virtually unassailable from any point within the discipline. Thus Rawls, summarizing his celebrated 'difference principle', writes that 'all social primary goods – liberty and opportunity, income and wealth, and the bases of self-respect – are to be distributed equally unless an unequal distribution of any or all of these goods is to the advantage of the least favoured'.[4] Ask the question 'Distributed by whom?' and you will search his book in vain for an answer. The state is omnipresent, all-possessing, all-powerful in organizing and distributing the social product, but never mentioned by name. The idea that wealth comes into the world already marked by claims of ownership, which can be cancelled only by violating the rights of individuals, is an idea that has no place in the left-liberal worldview.

It is precisely at this point that we should look for clear and transparent

---

4   *A Theory of Justice*, op. cit.

language in describing what is at stake. The socialist state does not 'redistribute' a common asset. It creates rents on the taxpayers' earnings, and offers those rents to its privileged clients. These clients hold on to their rents by voting for those who provide them.[5] If there are enough of their votes, the rents become a permanent possession of those fortunate enough to claim them. We then witness, as in Greece, the creation of a new 'leisure class', which uses the state in order to extract income from the remainder. At the same time the power of the state increases: when more than half the population is on the payroll of the state, as in France today, the social product is in effect confiscated from those who produce it and transferred to the bureaucracies who dispense it. And these bureaucracies become less and less accountable to the voters as their budget grows.

Those defects are serious enough. However, it seems to me that the real perversion of socialism is not to be found in the topsy-turvy economic theories that fascinated Marx, nor in the theories of social justice proposed by thinkers like John Rawls. The real perversion is a peculiar fallacy that sees life in society as one in which every success is someone else's failure. According to this fallacy, all gains are paid for by the losers. Society is a zero-sum game, in which costs and benefits balance out, and in which the winners' winning causes the losers' loss.

This 'zero sum' fallacy achieved a classic statement in Marx's theory of surplus value, which purported to show that the profit of the capitalist is confiscated from his workforce. Since all value originates in labour, some part of the value that the labourer produces is taken by the capitalist in the form of profit (or 'surplus value'). The labourer himself is compensated by a wage sufficient to 'reproduce his labour power'. But the 'surplus value' is retained by the capitalist. In short, all profits in the hands of the capitalist are losses inflicted on the labourer – a confiscation of 'hours of unpaid labour'.

That theory does not have many subscribers today. Whatever we think of free-market economics, it has at least persuaded us that not all transactions are zero-sum games. Consensual agreements benefit both parties: why else would they enter them? And that is as true of the wage contract as it is of any contract of sale. On the other hand, the zero-sum vision remains a potent component in socialist thinking, and a tried and trusted recourse in all the challenges offered

---

[5]   See James M. Buchanan, 'Rent-seeking, non-compensated transfer, and laws of succession,' *Journal of Law and Economics*, 26 April 1983: 71–85.

by reality. For a certain kind of temperament, defeat is never defeat by reality, but always defeat by other people, often acting together as members of a class, tribe, conspiracy or clan. Hence the unanswered and unanswerable complaint of so many socialists, who cannot admit that the poor benefit from the wealth of the wealthy. Injustice, for such people, is conclusively proved by inequality, so that the mere existence of a wealthy class justifies the plan to redistribute its assets among the 'losers'.

If you injure me, I have a grievance against you: I want justice, revenge, or at least an apology and an attempt to make amends. This kind of grievance is between you and me, and it might be the occasion of our coming closer together should the right moves be made. The zero-sum way of thinking is not like that. It does not begin from injury, but from disappointment. It looks around for some contrasting success, on which to pin its resentment. And only then does it work on proving to itself that the other's success was the cause of my failure. Those who have invested their hopes in some future state which will be one of blessedness will very often end up with transferable grievances of this kind, which they carry around, ready to attach to every observed contentment, and to hold the successful to account for their own otherwise inexplicable failure.

The Greeks believed that, by standing too vividly above the mediocre level permitted by the jealous gods, the big person provokes divine anger – such is the fault of *hubris*. Believing this, the Greeks could enjoy guilt-free resentment. They could send their distinguished citizens into exile, or put them to death, believing that in doing so they merely carried out the judgement of the gods. Thus the great general Aristides, who bore much of the responsibility for the victory over the Persians at Marathon and Salamis, and who was nicknamed 'the Just' on account of his exemplary and self-denying conduct, was ostracized and exiled by the citizens of Athens. It is reported by Plutarch that an illiterate voter who did not know Aristides came up to him and, giving him his voting shard, desired him to write upon it the name of Aristides. The latter asked if Aristides had wronged him. 'No,' was the reply, 'and I do not even know him, but I am tired of hearing him everywhere called, "The Just".' After hearing this, Aristides, being just, wrote his own name on the shard.

Cautious people may not agree with Nietzsche, that *ressentiment* is the bottom line of our social emotions. But they will recognize its ubiquity, and its propensity to bolster its hopes and feed its venom through self-serving applications of the zero-sum fallacy. Zero-sum ways of thinking seem to emerge spontaneously in modern communities, wherever the effects of competition and cooperation are felt. The Russian October Revolution did not target Kerensky's government only. It targeted the *successful*, those who had made a go of things, so as to stand out among their contemporaries. In every field and every institution, those at the top were identified, expropriated, murdered or sent into exile, with Lenin personally overseeing the removal of those whom he judged to be the best.[6] This, according to the zero-sum fallacy, was the way to improve the condition of the remainder. Stalin's targeting of the kulaks, the property-owning peasants, exemplified the same cast of mind, as did Hitler's targeting of the Jews, whose privileges and property had in Nazi eyes been purchased at the cost of the German working class. The explosion of anti-bourgeois sentiment in post-war France, leading to works like Sartre's *Saint Genet* and Simone de Beauvoir's *Second Sex*, followed the same logic, and was incorporated into the philosophy of the *soixante-huitards*.

It seems to me that this zero-sum fallacy underlies the widespread belief that equality and justice are the same idea – the belief that seems to be the default position of socialists, and programmed as such into university courses of political philosophy. Few people believe that if Jack has more money than Jill this is in itself a sign of injustice. But if Jack belongs to a *class* with money, and Jill to a class without it, then the zero-sum way of thinking immediately kicks in, to persuade people that Jack's class has become rich at the expense of Jill's. This is the impetus behind the Marxist theory of surplus value. But it is also one of the leading motives of social reform in our time, and one that is effectively undermining the real claims of justice and putting a spurious substitute in the place of them. For a certain kind of egalitarian mentality, it matters not that Jack has worked for his wealth and Jill merely lounged in voluntary idleness; it matters not that Jack has talent and energy, whereas Jill has neither; it matters not that Jack deserves what he has while Jill deserves nothing: the only important question is that of class, and the 'social' inequalities that stem from it. Concepts like right and desert fall out of the picture, and equality alone defines the goal.

The result has been the emergence in modern politics of a wholly novel idea of justice – one that has little or nothing to do with right, desert, reward or retribution, and which is effectively detached from the actions and responsibilities of individuals. This novel concept of justice (which, some would maintain, is

[6]   For an account of one extraordinary episode, see Lesley Chamberlain, *The Philosophy Steamer* (London: Atlantic Books, 2006).

not a concept of justice at all)[7] has governed educational reform in Western societies, and particularly in Britain, where long-term class resentments have found a voice in Parliament and a clear target in the schools. And the example is worth pondering, since it illustrates the near impossibility of escaping from zero-sum thinking.

I had the good fortune to gain entrance to our local grammar school – and thereby to work my way through the school to Cambridge University and an academic career. My grammar school, like many, had modelled itself on the public schools, adopting their curriculum, their style and some of their mannerisms. It aimed to provide for its pupils the very same opportunities that they might have had if their parents had been rich. And it succeeded. Those lucky enough to gain entrance to High Wycombe Royal Grammar School had an education as good as any then available, and the proof of this was that our old boys were represented among fellows of Cambridge colleges by a number second only to that achieved by Eton.

Those who collaborated in providing this opportunity to young people from poor backgrounds were acting from a sense of duty. But duties of charity are not duties of justice; if we fail to perform a duty of justice we commit an injustice – in other words, we wrong someone. The concept of justice is mediated by those of right and desert: the duty of justice is explicitly targeted at the other person, and takes account of his rights, his deserts and his valid claims. The concept of charity is not so explicitly targeted, and duties of charity have an open-ended character. If you extend charitable help to one person, and thereby exhaust your resources so that you cannot help another who is just as much in need of them, you do not wrong that second person. You have fulfilled your duty by offering help to the one who received it. To a certain extent the egalitarian outlook in politics stems from a suspicion of charity, and a desire to construe all duties as duties of justice, which cannot make arbitrary distinctions between those with an equal claim, when the only basis for that claim is need. As subsequent arguments will imply, that narrow conception of the realm of duty has proved to be fundamentally subversive of civic institutions.

The existence of the grammar schools arose from a long tradition of charitable giving (our school was founded in 1542), which was eventually subsumed within the state educational system. But a procedure that enables some pupils

---

[7] On this point, see Patrick Burke, *The Concept of Justice: Is Social Justice Just?* (London: Continuum, 2011).

to succeed must cause others to fail: so the zero-sum fallacy maintains. Such a procedure therefore generates a 'two-tier' education system, with the successful enjoying all the opportunities, and the failures left by the wayside to be 'marked for life'. In other words, the success of some is paid for by the failure of others. Justice requires that the opportunities be equalized. Thus was born the movement for comprehensive education, together with the hostility to streaming, and the downgrading of examinations, in order to prevent the state education system from producing and reproducing 'inequalities'.

It is easy to ensure equality in the field of education: it suffices to remove all the opportunities for getting ahead, so that no child ever succeeds in learning anything. And to the cynical observer this is what happened. It is no part of my purpose to endorse that cynicism, though it has many times been expressed during the years since Anthony Crosland and Shirley Williams, education ministers under Labour governments, set out to destroy the grammar schools.[8] I wish simply to offer an illustration of the zero-sum fallacy at work. A system that offered to children from poor families an opportunity to advance by talent and industry alone was destroyed for the simple reason that it divided the successes from the failures. Of course it is a tautology to say that examinations divide successes from failures, and it can hardly be a requirement of justice to abolish that distinction. But the new concept of 'social' justice came to the rescue of the egalitarians, and enabled them to present their malice towards the successful as a kind of compassion towards the rest.

A dose of realism reminds us that human beings are diverse, and that a child might fail at one thing while succeeding at another. Only a diverse educational system, with well-designed and rigorous examinations, will enable children to find the skill, expertise or vocation that suits their abilities. Zero-sum thinking, which sees the educational success of one child as paid for by the failure of another, forces education into a mould that is alien to it. The child who fails at Latin might succeed at music or metalwork; the one who fails to get to university might succeed as an army officer. We all know this, and it is as true of educational procedures as it is true of markets, that they are not zero-sum games. Yet that is how they are treated, whenever false hopes are invested in the utopian idea of 'education for equality'. The routine among politicians and

---

[8]   For example by Kingsley Amis and others in the 'Black Papers' on education, the first of which was C. B. Cox and A. E. Dyson (eds), *Fight for Education* (London: Critical Quarterly Society, 1969).

educational experts is to hunt out places of excellence – Oxbridge, the public schools, the grammar schools, choir schools – and find ways to penalize them or to close them down. That way, the fallacy tells us, the others will benefit, and we will at last have an educational system that conforms to the requirements of 'social justice'.

Rejection of zero-sum thinking and the associated concept of 'social justice' does not mean accepting inequality in its current form. We can question the idea of social justice without believing that all inequalities are just. Besides, inequality breeds resentment, and resentment must be overcome if there is to be social harmony. Wealthy people may be aware of this and anxious to do something about it. They may give to charity, devote some part of their resources to helping others, and in general display an appropriate measure of sympathy for those less fortunate than themselves. In particular, they may set up enterprises that offer employment, and so give to others a stake in their own success. That is how it has usually been in America, and it is one reason why, in my experience, Americans, however disadvantaged, are pleased by others' good fortune – believing that, in some way, they might have a share in it.

In European countries, however, it is not normal for people to be pleased by the good fortune of others. We are often afraid to reveal our wealth, our power or our success in worldly things, for fear of the aggression that this will attract. Nietzsche attributed *ressentiment* to a deep fault in our civilization, manifested equally in the Christian religion, in democracy and in the socialist programmes of his day. Max Scheler, defending Christianity against Nietzsche's charge, was more disposed to attribute resentment to bourgeois morality, which measures everything in terms of material possessions.[9] Socialism, for Scheler, was just the latest form that this morality had taken. And there is no doubt that resentment has played an important role in the attitude to inequality that prevails today. I see no solution to widespread resentment other than the traditional American one – to put your wealth to use, and to give as many people as possible an interest in your using it successfully, meanwhile adopting those 'envy-avoiding stratagems' explored by Helmut Schoeck.[10] But things have changed in ways that threaten the old American model. There has been, both before and after the financial

[9] Max Scheler, *Ressentiment*, 1912–1915, available as free download from www.scribd.com (accessed 1 February 2014).
[10] Helmut Schoeck, *Envy: A Theory of Social Behaviour*, Liberty Fund, also a download from Mises.org (accessed 1 February 2014).

crisis of 2008, a sudden and escalating rise in the disparity between incomes at the top end of the scale and those at the bottom. This has happened all across the developed world, and in America in particular. Joseph Stiglitz has argued that the top percentile of Americans has increased in wealth not only while those lower down the scale have either remained static or fallen into poverty, but more importantly that the wealth of those at the top has been increased at the cost of those beneath them.[11] If this were true, then any policy to relieve poverty must also address the problem of inequality, achieving some redistribution of wealth at the expense of those who currently possess it. I do not know whether Stiglitz's conclusion is true, however. For there is a covert use of the zero-sum fallacy in the arguments that he gives for it. If wealthy people get wealthier at a time when the poor get poorer, it does not follow that the losses of the poor are *transferred* as profits to the rich. Unless we establish causality here we cannot be sure that a policy designed to equalize rich and poor would, in the long run, benefit anyone.

I have argued that we must distinguish the core of truth in socialism, which tells us that we enjoy the fruits of society only if we are also ready to share them, from the casing of resentment that surrounds it. As with nationalism, the core of truth has been exaggerated into heresy, so changing truth to error, and natural sentiment to religious need. There is a temptation, felt most strongly by left-wing intellectuals, to replace the imperfect individual with the pure abstraction, to rewrite the human world as though it were composed of forces, movements, classes and ideas, all moving in a stratosphere of historical necessity from which the messy realities have been excluded. This Orwell perceived in the world that the intellectuals had created – the world dreamed up and imposed by the Communist Party and distilled in the 'Ingsoc' of *Nineteen Eighty-Four*. As a call to rectify the existing order, socialism should appeal to us all. But as an attempt to revise human nature, and to conscript us in the pursuit of the millennium, it was a dangerous fantasy, an attempt to realize heaven that would lead inevitably to hell. We can see this clearly now, as the Western world emerges from the Cold War and the communist nightmare. But still the 'totalitarian temptation', as Jean-François Revel called it, is there – the temptation to remake society, so that equality is imposed from above by the benign socialist state, whose good intentions can never be questioned since nobody knows what it would be like to achieve them.[12]

[11] Joseph Stiglitz, *The Price of Inequality* (New York: W. W Norton, 2012).
[12] Jean-François Revel, *La Tentation totalitaire* (Paris: Robert Laffont, 1976).

5

The Truth in Capitalism

The term 'capitalism' entered European languages through the writings of the French utopian philosopher, Saint-Simon. It was picked up by Marx to denote the institutionalized private ownership of the 'means of production'. Marx contrasted capitalism with other economic 'systems' – notably with slavery, feudalism and socialism – and predicted that, just as capitalism had overthrown feudalism in a violent revolution, so would capitalism be overthrown by socialism. In due course, socialism would 'wither away', to leave the 'full communism' that lies at the end of history. The theory is unbelievable, its predictions false, and its legacy appalling. Nevertheless, its terms changed the language of political debate in the nineteenth century, and we are now stuck with them. The word 'capitalism' is still used to describe any economy based on private property and free exchange. And the term 'socialism' is still used to denote the various attempts to limit, control or replace some aspect of capitalism, so understood. In all its appearances, therefore, capitalism, like socialism, is a matter of degree.

It is important to be aware of terms that have been inherited from dead theories. They may have an aura of authority, but they also distort our perceptions and weigh down our consciousness with newspeak, of the kind so brilliantly satirized by George Orwell in *Nineteen Eighty-Four*. Orwell's point in writing that book was to show that the dehumanizing jargon of Marxism produces also a dehumanized world, in which people become abstractions, and truth is merely an instrument in the hands of power. And the point should never be forgotten by conservatives, who need to escape from the nineteenth-century theories that sought to make their position not just obsolete but also, in some way, inexpressible. We need to look at the world afresh, using the natural language of human relations.

That said, it would be foolish and naïve to assume that the attacks levelled at something called 'capitalism' are without foundation, or do not need a reply. In order to develop this reply we need to begin from the *truth* in capitalism, the truth that socialism has traditionally denied. And this truth is simple, namely that private ownership and free exchange are necessary features of any large-scale economy – any economy in which people depend for their survival and prosperity on the activities of strangers. It is only when people have rights of property, and can freely exchange what they own for what they need, that a society of strangers can achieve economic coordination. Socialists don't in their hearts accept this. They see society as a mechanism for distributing resources among those with a claim to them, as though resources all exist in advance of the activities that create them, and as though there is a way to determine exactly who has a right to what, without reference to the long history of economic cooperation.

The point was brought home by the Austrian economists – notably by von Mises and Hayek – during the 'calculation debate' that surrounded the early proposals for a socialist economy, in which prices and production would both be controlled by the state. The Austrian response to these proposals turns on three crucial ideas. First, economic activity depends upon knowledge of other people's wants, needs and resources. Second, this knowledge is dispersed throughout society and is not the property of any individual. Third, in the free exchange of goods and services, the price mechanism provides access to this knowledge – not as a theoretical statement, but as a signal to action. Prices in a free economy offer the solution to countless simultaneous equations mapping individual demand against available supply.

When production and distribution are fixed by a central authority, however, prices no longer provide an index either of the scarcity of a resource or of the extent of others' demand for it. The crucial piece of economic knowledge, which exists in the free economy as a social fact, has been destroyed. The economy either breaks down, with queues, gluts and shortages replacing the spontaneous order of distribution, or is replaced by a black economy in which things exchange at their real price – the price that people are prepared to pay for them.[1] This result has been abundantly confirmed by the experience of socialist

---

[1]   The argument that I have here condensed is spelled out in detail in Ludwig von Mises, *Socialism: An Economic and Sociological Analysis*, trans. J. Kahane (London: Jonathan Cape, 1936 [first published 1922 as *Die Gemeinwirtschaft: Untersuchungen über den Sozialismus*] and in the essays in Hayek's *Individualism and Economic Order* (London and Chicago: University of Chicago Press, 1948), especially the three essays on 'Socialist Calculation' there reprinted.

economies; however, the argument given in support of it is not empirical but *a priori*. It is based on broad philosophical conceptions concerning socially generated and socially dispersed information.

The important point in the argument is that the price of a commodity conveys reliable economic information only if the economy is free. It is only in conditions of free exchange that the budgets of individual consumers feed into the epistemic process, as one might call it, which distils in the form of price the collective solution to their shared economic problem – the problem of knowing what to produce, and what to exchange for it. All attempts to interfere with this process, by controlling either the supply or the price of a product, will lead to a loss of economic knowledge. For that knowledge is not contained in a plan, but only in the economic activity of free agents, as they produce, market and exchange their goods according to the laws of supply and demand. The planned economy, which offers a rational distribution in place of the 'random' distribution of the market, destroys the information on which the proper functioning of an economy depends. It therefore undermines its own knowledge base. It is a supreme example of a project that is supposedly rational while not being rational at all, since it depends on knowledge that is available only in conditions that it destroys.

One corollary of this argument is that economic knowledge, of the kind contained in prices, lives in the system, is generated by the free activity of countless rational choosers and cannot be translated into a set of propositions or fed as premises into some problem-solving device. As the Austrians were possibly the first to realize, economic activity displays the peculiar logic of collective action, when the response of one person changes the information base of another. Out of this recognition grew the science of game theory, developed by von Neumann and Morgenstern as a first step towards an explanation of markets, but pursued today as a branch of mathematics with applications (and misapplications) in every area of social and political life.[2]

Hayek's epistemic theory of the market does not claim that the market is the only form of spontaneous order, nor that a free market is *sufficient* to produce either economic coordination or social stability. The theory asserts only that the price mechanism generates and contains knowledge that is *necessary* to economic coordination. Coordination can be defeated by business cycles,

---

[2]   J. von Neumann and O. Morgenstern, *The Theory of Games and Economic Behaviour* (Princeton, NJ: Princeton University Press, 1944).

market failures and externalities, and is in any case dependent on other forms of spontaneous order for its long-term survival. John O'Neill, defending a mitigated socialism against Hayek's advocacy of the free economy, argues that the price mechanism does not communicate all the information necessary to economic coordination, and that in any case information is not enough.[3] There are good conservative reasons for agreeing with O'Neill's claims; but they are reasons that Hayek accepts. The market is held in place by other forms of spontaneous order, not all of which are to be understood simply as epistemic devices, but some of which – moral and legal traditions, for example – create the kind of solidarity that markets, left to themselves, will erode.

Implicit in Hayek is the thought that free exchange and enduring customs are to be justified in exactly the same terms. Both are indispensable distillations of socially necessary knowledge, the one operating synchronously, the other diachronically, in order to bring the experiences of indefinitely many others to bear on the decision taken by me, here, now. Hayek emphasizes the free market as part of a wider spontaneous order founded in the free exchange of goods, ideas and interests – the 'game of catallaxy' as he calls it.[4] But this game is played over time, and – to adapt a thought of Burke's – the dead and the unborn are also players, who make their presence known not through markets, but through traditions, institutions and laws.

Those who believe that social order should place constraints on the market are therefore right. But in a true spontaneous order the constraints are already there, in the form of customs, laws and morals. If those good things decay, then there is no way, according to Hayek, that legislation can replace them. For they arise spontaneously or not at all, and the imposition of legislative edicts for the 'good society' may threaten what remains of the accumulated wisdom that makes such a society possible. Instead of constraining our activity into the channels required by justice – which is the task of the common law – social legislation imposes a set of goals. It turns law into an instrument of social engineering, and allows utilitarian thinking to override the claims of natural right. In emergencies, or in conditions of manifest disequilibrium, legislation might be the only weapon we have. But we should always remember that legislation does not create a legal order but presupposes it, and that in our case – the

---

[3]   John O'Neill, *Market: Ethics, Knowledge and Politics* (London: Routledge, 1998), pp. 134ff.
[4]   *Law, Legislation and Liberty*, vol. 2, pp. 108–9.

case of the anglosphere – the legal order arose by an invisible hand from the attempt to do justice in individual conflicts.

In other words, legal order arose spontaneously, and not through a rational plan, just as the economic order did. We should not be surprised therefore if British conservative thinkers – notably Hume, Smith, Burke and Oakeshott – have tended to see no tension between a defence of the free market and a traditionalist vision of social order. For they have put their faith in the spontaneous limits placed on the market by the moral consensus of the community and have seen both the market and the constraints as the work of the same invisible hand. Maybe that moral consensus is now breaking down. But the breakdown is in part the result of state interference, and certainly unlikely to be cured by it.

It is at this point, however, that conservatives may wish to enter a note of caution. Although Hayek may be right in believing that the free market and traditional morality are both forms of spontaneous order and both to be justified epistemically, it does not follow that the two will not conflict. Socialists are not alone in pointing to the corrosive effects of markets on the forms of human settlement, or in emphasizing the distinction between things with a value and things with a price. Indeed, many of the traditions to which conservatives are most attached can be understood (from the point of view of Hayek's 'evolutionary rationality') as devices for rescuing human life from the market. Traditional sexual morality, for example, which insists on the sanctity of the human person, the sacramental character of marriage, and the sinfulness of sex outside the vow of love, is – seen from the Hayekian perspective – a way of taking sex off the market, of refusing it the status of a commodity and ring-fencing it against exchange. This practice has an evident social function; but it is a function that can be fulfilled only if people see sex as a realm of intrinsic values and sexual prohibitions as absolute commands. In all societies, religion, which emerges spontaneously, is connected to such ideas of non-negotiable order. To put the matter succinctly, that is sacred which does not have a price. And a concern for the priceless and the non-exchangeable is exactly what defines the conservative view of society, as I described it in Chapter 2.

It follows that the 'game of catallaxy' does not provide a complete account of politics, nor does it resolve the question of how and to what extent the state might choose to interfere in the market, in order to give the advantage to some other and potentially conflicting form of spontaneous order, or in order to correct the negative side effects to which all human cooperation is liable. This question defines the point where conservatism and socialism meet and also the nature of the conflict between them. The truth in capitalism – that private property under a rule of free exchange is the only way to manage economic cooperation in a society of strangers – does not answer the critics of capitalism, whose target is not the free economy but the distortions that arise within it, and which breed resentment and distrust among the losers.

The most important lesson to take, both from Adam Smith's original defence of the free economy, as the beneficent working of the 'invisible hand', and from Hayek's defence of spontaneous order as the vehicle of economic information, is that a free economy is an economy run by free beings. And free beings are responsible beings. Economic transactions in a regime of private property depend not only on distinguishing mine from yours, but also on relating me to you. Without accountability, nobody is to be trusted, and without trust the virtues that are attributed to the free economy would not arise. Every transaction in the market takes time, and in the time between initiation and completion only trust, not ownership, holds things in place.

That, perhaps, is obvious. It is somewhat less obvious that trustworthy beings emerge only in certain circumstances, and that trust can be as easily eroded by a free economy as sustained by it. No market economy can function properly without the support of legal and moral sanctions, designed to hold individual agents to their bargains, and to return the cost of misbehaviour to the one who causes it. But modern economies have developed ways of avoiding costs or passing them on that effectively remove the sanctions from dishonest or manipulative behaviour. The economies considered by Adam Smith and his nineteenth-century successors were economies in which the assets owned by the parties were items of real property for which the owner took full responsibility, and which were looked after by those who owned them. The house, horse or haystack had been maintained by the seller, who was responsible for the condition in which he or she passed it to the buyer. But with the growth of modern financial markets all kinds of things exchange on the market that have no such tangible reality in the lives of those who deal in them, and which are exchanged quickly before any liability for their condition can easily arise. We saw this with the sub-prime mortgage crisis in America, in which banks traded in debts that they could not guarantee and which no one else could guarantee either; we see it in the hedge fund market, in which managers trade in bets taken by others on activities that no party to the transaction controls. And this trade in 'unreal estate' is often conducted by spectral entities that exist nowhere in particular, vanishing from the places where they might be held accountable as soon as an investigation or a tax demand looks likely, to reappear on some distant horizon, claiming immunity from all the charges that might be made against them.

This dealing in phantoms provokes strong reactions. Surely it must be dishonest; or if not dishonest then massively unfair, a way of taxing the economy without making a contribution to it, and a way of both creating and exploiting disequilibrium, so as to cream off vast profits while others are forced to make equivalent losses.

Is that criticism just? Is it another appearance of the zero-sum fallacy that I dismissed in the previous chapter? Is it, perhaps, the latest form taken by the age-old condemnation of 'usury', which saw interest, insurance and the market in futures as ways of taxing other people's honest labour without contributing to the product? It is hard to say, since so much of the modern economy seems to depend upon intricate financial instruments deployed in ways for which there is little or no precedent. It is natural, in response, to sympathize with current attempts at 'Islamic banking', in which the Prophet's condemnation of interest, insurance and the other ways of dealing in 'unreal estate' is built into the ways of saving and investing. But the resulting system proves to be elaborately dependent on legal fictions (*hiyal*) which resurrect the problem all over again, by making unreal estate into the primary subject-matter of financial contracts.[5] It seems to me that there is no alternative but to bite the bullet and accept that the new financial instruments are a natural extension of market principles into realms that have yet to be fully explored. To say that the use of these instruments is always dishonest is to deprive us of the very real distinction we need to make, between those who deal openly and honestly with these unreal assets, and those whose intention is to exploit and deceive.

Conservatives believe in private property because they respect the autonomy of the individual. But it is fair to say that too many conservatives have failed to take seriously the many abuses to which property is subject. Libertarian economists have rightly emphasized the role of the market in spreading freedom and prosperity, and have shown clearly that the wage contract is not, as Marx

---

[5]   See Nabil Saleh, *Unlawful Gain and Legitimate Profit in Islamic Law: Riba, Gharar, and Islamic Banking* (Cambridge: Cambridge University Press, 1986).

supposed, a zero-sum game, in which one party gains what the other loses, but an arrangement for mutual benefit. But the market is the benign mechanism that Hayek and others describe only when it is constrained by an impartial rule of law, and only when all participants bear the costs of their actions as well as reaping the benefits.

Unfortunately, that idealized vision of the market is increasingly far from the truth. Certainly, at the local level, private deals have all the beneficial and freedom-enhancing characteristics that the libertarians emphasize. But as soon as we rise above that level, to consider the activities of the larger corporations, the picture changes. Instead of the benign competition to secure a market share, we discover a malign competition to externalize costs. The firm that can transfer its costs to others has the advantage over the one that must meet its costs itself, and if the costs can be transferred so widely that it is impossible to identify a victim, they can be effectively written off.

To take a simple example, consider the bottle. Bottles used to be comparatively expensive to produce, and when I was a child the manufacturers of bottled drinks would charge two pence for the bottle. This charge would be refunded when the bottle was returned to the shop, to be collected for re-use by the manufacturer. Two pence was then a lot of money – about half the cost of the drink. Nobody threw bottles away, and all were recycled. Nowhere in the verges or along railways lines would you ever see the gleam of castaway glass. Our world was rimmed with grass, not glass; grass hemmed the roads, tumbled down the banks of railway cuttings and was never disturbed except by footprints.

Now that bottles can be cheaply produced in both glass and plastic, a manufacturer finds that it costs less to abandon them to their fate than to reclaim them. This practice has huge environmental and social consequences. But they are not borne by the manufacturer, and are distributed so widely that no particular group is singled out as the victim. We are as yet living in the early years of non-biodegradable packaging. But already many parts of England's once beautiful countryside are awash with plastic bottles, cups and sandwich wraps, which clog the streams and ditches, block the drains, exacerbate floods, pose a threat to farming and wildlife, and rub out a national icon, with incalculable effects on the sense of community.

Why do the defenders of the market not raise their voices against the practice of externalizing costs in that way? After all, to pass on your costs without accounting for them is not merely to impose them on others; it is to destroy the process of reward and penalty whereby the market realizes its potential as a self-regulating device. The ease with which large producers can transfer their costs is the glaring abuse through which the market – otherwise one of the core values of conservatism – condemns itself.

When Disraeli first saw that private property was an integral part of the conservative cause, to be defended with all possible vigour against the socialists, he added an important qualification, which he called 'the feudal principle', that the *right* of property is also a *duty*. The one who enjoys property is also accountable for it, and in particular accountable to those upon whom it might otherwise impose a burden. He has responsibilities towards the less fortunate, towards the unborn, and towards the inheritance in which we all have a stake. Disraeli's concern was directed to the condition of the new urban working class, and environmental problems were not high on his political agenda. But today they are at the top of everyone's agenda, and there is no conceivable chance that the conservative defence of property will gain converts among the young without the attempt to show that it is not state control but private ownership that will save the planet from human waste. I therefore return to this problem in Chapter 8 below.

Whole branches of the modern economy have grown from the practice of transferring costs. The most conspicuous example is the supermarket. A great many of the costs incurred by the large-scale centralization of food distri-bution in the supermarket chains are met by the taxpayer. Transport networks built at public expense, and zoning laws favouring shopping malls and large warehouses, give supermarkets an insuperable advantage over their high-street competitors. At the same time there are enormous environmental and aesthetic costs to this extensive distribution network. These less tangible costs are also met by the general public, which will have the long-term responsibility of dealing with the ever-expanding sprawl and the effects of energy-dependence. To those burdens we must add the cost of the packaging, which constitutes 25 per cent by weight of the products passing the supermarket till. Most of this packaging is non-degradable, and exists in order to promote the economies of scale that enable supermarkets to undercut the grocery stores that are their only real competitors.

In those and a multitude of other ways the supermarkets have succeeded in externalizing the real cost of their success – success in eliminating local stores, in compelling people to drive to the mall for their provisions, in distributing cheap food to every part of the country without the trouble of dealing with local producers or without paying the real cost of its production. A similar story can be told about most other chain stores in Europe and America. It can be told about the building materials industry, about the manufacturers of soft drinks and candies, about the makers and distributors of tools and hardware. In short, global capitalism is in some respects less an exercise in free market economics, in which cost is assumed for the sake of benefit, than a kind of brigandage, in which costs are transferred to future generations for the sake of rewards here and now. How do we restore the 'feudal principle' to an economy that has moved so far in this direction? That ought to be a major and troubling item on the conservative agenda. But it is all but unmentionable in political debates either in America or in Europe. Even socialists steer away from any criticism of the *real* corporate predation, which is the predation on future generations in which we too are involved. Like the elites of New Labour and the German Social Democrat Party, they live in the same way as the CEOs with whom they frequently associate, transferring the costs of their policies to future governments, in just the way that the corporations transfer the costs of their economic success to the unborn.

The best hope, it seems to me, is the emergence of a new form of conservatism, which – like that promoted by Disraeli – would be concerned to defend private property against those who abuse it, and to secure the freedom of the present generation without cost to the next. It could not possibly give more than two cheers – and maybe less than two – to the global economy, to the World Trade Organization (WTO), or to the new kind of lawless capitalism exemplified by China. And it would present to the people of the Western democracies a model of responsible business, in which small initiatives, responsible accounting, and local ties are given the place that they deserve – the place without which the market will not return to equilibrium, but proceed helter-skelter towards environmental catastrophe.

I return to the problem of externalities in Chapter 8, below. But there is another issue that conservatives need here to address. The appeal of Marxism no longer resides in the theory of exploitation, or the promise of revolution or the critique of the bourgeoisie. It resides in the analysis of 'commodity fetishism' in Volume One of *Das Kapital*, an analysis that is the ancestor of a continuing criticism of markets and which ultimately derives from the Old Testament diatribes against idolatry. The complaint is made that the market uproots human appetite, puts on sale even those things that should not be exchanged except as a gift, endows everything with a price, and leads us into a world of transitory illusions and false representations, an 'aestheticized' world, so enslaving us through our own manufactured cravings.[6]

The criticism has been made in many ways and in many tones of voice, but always it centres on the distinction between true desires, that lead to fulfilment of the one who satisfies them, from false desires, which are 'temptations', leading to the disruption, alienation and fragmentation of the self. That distinction lies at the heart of religion and is the theme of much serious art. It needs to be acknowledged, especially now that we live in a time of abundance. Material values, idolatry and sensory indulgence are steadily eroding our awareness that there really are goods that cannot be put on sale, since to do so is to destroy them – goods like love, sex, beauty and settlement. These goods are not fully understood in advance of receiving them, nor can we quantify them or enter them into some cost-benefit equation.[7] They emerge through our associations and exist by being shared. In the penultimate chapter, therefore, I return to these goods, in order to show just why it is that they have no place in the life of *Homo oeconomicus*.

For all the good sense that lies at the heart of that argument, however, it seems to me that we should hesitate before accepting that the distinction between true and false desires, which belongs to the moral life and which all parents have a duty to teach to their children, is threatened by a market economy. Markets put things on sale – that is true. But the decision to fence the things that are not to be sold is ours, to be made by law when it is not made by agreement. Given that there is no alternative to a market economy, the only question is how to withhold from it the things that are not to be sold. This is not a political question only. It concerns education, custom, culture and the workings of civil society, as well as the decisions of a legislature.

We cannot now escape from the 'commodification' of life that prosperity has naturally brought to us. But we can strive to discipline it through good taste,

---

[6] For the latest version of this never-ending critique, see Gilles Lipovetsky and Jean Serroy, *L'esthétisation du monde: vivre à l'âge du capitalisme artiste* (Paris: Gallimard 2013). Previous versions of the critique enrolled Thorstein Veblen, Theodor Adorno, Herbert Marcuse, Vance Packard, J. K. Galbraith, Naomi Klein … and a hundred more.

[7] Needless to say, there are mad economists who show us how to price these priceless things. For a particularly absurd instance, see Richard Posner, *Sex and Reason* (Cambridge, MA: Harvard University Press, 1992). For a general criticism, see Philip Roscoe, *I Spend Therefore I Am* (London: Viking, 2014).

the love of beauty and the sense of decorum. Those good things don't come to us through politics: certainly not through politics of a liberal or socialist kind. It is futile to look for a political remedy to evils that we can address only if we can take advantage of the social cohesion that depends in its turn upon markets. Looking back on nationalism and socialism, as I described them in the previous two chapters, we should acknowledge that their worst forms arise when their adherents look to them to provide the equivalent of a religious faith – an absolute submission that will sweep away all doubt, demand total sacrifice and offer redemption in exchange. It is some such alternative to the realm of commodities that the latter-day Marxists are demanding. For what, after all, is the remedy to fetishism, if it is not the 'true religion' that puts the unknowable transcendence in place of the perceivable idol?

It is at this point that we must acknowledge the great value of liberalism, which, since its birth at the Enlightenment, has striven to impress upon us the radical distinction between religious and political order, and the need to build the art of government without depending upon the law of God.

6

The Truth in Liberalism

The word 'liberal' has changed meaning many times. It is now used in America to denote those who would be described as 'on the left' in European terms – people who believe that the state must use its powers and its resources to equalize the fates of its citizens, and who accept a larger role for the state in the economy and in the regulation of ordinary life than would be naturally endorsed by conservatives. But this use of the term 'liberal' is virtually the opposite of its use during the nineteenth century, when liberal parties set out to propagate the message that political order exists to guarantee individual freedom, and that authority and coercion can be justified only if liberty requires them. In this chapter I want to spell out the truth in liberalism, conceived in that way, as the philosophy that supposes the freedom of the individual to be one of the purposes, maybe the prime purpose, of government, and in pursuing that purpose distinguishes political from religious forms of social order.

The religious form of social order is laid before us in the Hebrew Bible and in the Koran: it is an order in which laws are based on divine prescriptions, and earthly offices are held by delegation from the Deity. Looked at from the outside, religions are defined by the communities who adopt them, and their function is to bind those communities together, to secure them against external shock, and to guarantee the course of reproduction. A religion is founded in piety, which is the habit of submitting to divine commands. This habit, once installed, underpins all oaths and promises, gives sanctity to marriage and upholds the sacrifices that are needed both in peace and in war. Hence communities with a shared religion have an advantage in the fight for land, and all the settled territories of our planet are places where some dominant religion has once staked out and defended its claims. Such is the story recounted in the Old Testament.

The political order, by contrast, is one in which a community is governed by man-made laws and human decisions, without reference to divine commands. Religion is a static condition; politics a dynamic process. While religions demand unquestioning submission, the political process offers participation, discussion and law-making founded in consent. So it has been in the Western tradition, and it is largely thanks to liberalism that this tradition has been maintained, in the face of the constant temptation, which we are seeing in its most vociferous form among Islamists today, to renounce the arduous task of compromise, and to take refuge in a regime of unquestionable commands.

The contest between religion and politics is not in itself a modern one. This we know not only from the Bible, but also from Greek tragedy. The action of Sophocles' *Antigone* hinges on the conflict between political order, represented and upheld by Creon, and religious duty, in the person of Antigone. The first is public, involving the whole community; the second is private, involving Antigone alone. Hence the conflict cannot be resolved. Public interest has no bearing on Antigone's decision to bury her dead brother, while the duty laid by divine command on Antigone cannot possibly be a reason for Creon to jeopardize the state.

A similar conflict informs the *Oresteia* of Aeschylus, in which a succession of religious murders, beginning with Agamemnon's ritual sacrifice of his daughter, lead at last to the terrifying persecution of Orestes by the furies. The gods demand the murders; the gods also punish them. Religion binds the house of Atreus, but in dilemmas that it does not resolve. Resolution comes at last only when judgement is handed over to the city, personified in Athena. In the political order, we are led to understand, justice replaces vengeance, and negotiated solutions abolish absolute commands. The message of the *Oresteia* resounds down the centuries of Western civilization: it is through politics, not religion, that peace is secured. Vengeance is mine, saith the Lord; but justice, says the city, is mine.

The Greek tragedians wrote at the beginning of Western civilization. But their world is continuous with our world. Their law is the law of the city, in which political decisions are arrived at by discussion, participation and dissent. It was in the context of the Greek city-state that political philosophy began, and the great questions of justice, authority and the constitution are discussed by Plato and Aristotle in terms that are current today. Liberalism arose from the centuries-long reflection on what is necessary, if people are to be governed by consent, so as willingly to submit to laws made by other humans rather than by God.

A society governed by consent does not necessarily issue from a social contract, whether actual or implied. It is a society in which dealings between citizens, and between citizens and those in authority, are consensual, in the manner of daily courtesies, games of football, theatrical events or family meals. As Adam Smith made clear, order may emerge from consensual dealings. But it emerges 'by an invisible hand', and not, as a rule, because someone has imposed it. In the previous chapter I mentioned Hayek's defence of the common law, expounded in *Law, Legislation and Liberty*, in which he argues that law, too, emerges from our free transactions, not because it is imposed, but because it is *implicit in our dealings*. The common law summarizes what reasonable beings already assume, whether or not explicitly, when they engage in free transactions. The principle of tort, that the wrongdoer must compensate the victim; the principle of contract, that the one who breaks the contract must compensate the other for his loss; the principle of equity, that he who seeks equity should do equity – all such principles are assumed in the very fact of free agreement. The common law arises from their application in particular cases, leading to remedies and rules through which we, free and accountable beings, can negotiate our position in a world of strangers.

A consensual order is one in which the decisions on which our relations with others depend are, discounting emergencies, freely taken. Decisions are free when each of us settles his path through life by negotiation, playing his cards according to his own best judgement and without coercion from others. Traditional liberalism is the view that such a society is possible only if the individual members have sovereignty over their own lives – which means being free both to grant and to withhold consent respecting whatever relations may be proposed to them. Individual sovereignty exists only where the state guarantees rights, such as the right to life, limb and property, so protecting citizens from invasion and coercion by others, including invasion and coercion by the state.

In discussion of these issues it is common to make a distinction between the subject and the citizen. Both subject and citizen are under an obligation of obedience towards the law and the state that enforces it. But while the obedience of subjects is unqualified, and demanded by the state without offering terms in exchange, the obedience of citizens is conditional on respect for their sovereignty. Citizenship is the condition of people living in a consensual society of sovereign individuals. It is a precious achievement of Western civilization, not observable everywhere in the world today, and largely misunderstood by Islamists, who envisage a form of perfect and unquestioning obedience to a law laid down by God, on the part of subjects who have renounced forever their freedom to dissent from it.

A modern democracy is perforce a society of strangers. And the successful democracy is the one where strangers are expressly included in the web of obligation. Citizenship involves the disposition to recognize and act upon obligations to those whom we do not know. It enables strangers to stand side by side against authority and to assert their common rights. It therefore provides a shield against oppression and an echo to the dissenting voice. Without this recourse there is no outlet for opposition, except through a conspiracy to subvert the ruling power. Those thoughts are already incipient in the writ of *Habeas corpus*.

Western democracies did not create the virtue of citizenship; on the contrary, they grew from it. Nothing is more evident in *The Federalist* than the public spirit that it puts in play, in opposition to factions, cabals and private scheming. As Madison pointed out, democratic elections do not suffice to overcome faction, or to instil a true sense of public answerability into the hearts of those who are elected. Only in a republic – a system of representational offices filled by citizens held answerable to those who elected them – will true patriotism animate the workings of power.[1] The Constitution of the United States was successful largely because those who devised it sought to found a republic in which the obligation to strangers would find concrete embodiment in the institutions of the Union: a republic in which factions would have only social, rather than political, power. Democracy was adopted as a means to this goal; but it is a dangerous means, and depends upon maintaining the public spirit of the citizens if it is not to degenerate into a battle-ground for special interests.

It is characteristic of the times in which we live, to identify the virtue of citizenship with the democratic spirit, so encouraging the belief that the good citizen is simply the person who puts all questions to the vote. On the contrary, the good citizen is the one who knows when voting is the *wrong* way to decide a question, as well as when voting is the right way. For he knows that his obligations to strangers may be violated when majority opinion alone decides their fate. That is part of what Tocqueville and Mill had in mind when warning us against the tyranny of the majority.[2] Political order enables us to transcend the rule of the majority. And the great gift of political liberalism to Western

[1] See James Madison, *The Federalist*, no. 10, in George W. Carey and James McClellan (eds), *The Federalist* (Dubuque, IA: Kendall/Hunt, 1990), pp. 46–9.

[2] Alexis de Tocqueville, *Democracy in America*, trans. and eds Harvey Mansfield and Delba Winthrop (Chicago: University of Chicago Press, 2000); John Stuart Mill, *Of Representative Government* (London: Parker Son and Bourn, 1861).

civilization has been in working out the conditions under which protection is offered to the dissident, and religious unity replaced by rational discussion among opponents.

In Western democracies our governments are aware that many people, perhaps even a majority, did not vote for them, and that they must therefore make themselves acceptable to people with whom they disagree. Of course, there are aspects of human life in which compromise is either suspect or forbidden. In battle you don't compromise with the enemy. In religion you don't compromise with the devil. But it is precisely when religion intrudes into politics that the political process is most at risk. This is the reason why, in the history of modern Egypt, successive presidents have tried to keep the Muslim Brotherhood out of power. The Brotherhood believes that law and politics are not about compromise but about obedience to the unalterable will of God.

In the seventeenth century, Britain was torn apart by civil war, and at the heart of that civil war was religion – the Puritan desire to impose godly rule on the people of Great Britain regardless of whether they wanted it, and the leaning of the Stuart Kings towards a Roman Catholic faith that had become deeply antipathetic to the majority and a vehicle for unwanted foreign interference. In a civil war both sides behave badly, precisely because the spirit of compromise has fled from the scene. The solution is not to impose a new set of decrees from on high, but to re-establish the legitimacy of opposition and the politics of compromise. This was recognized at the Glorious Revolution of 1688, when Parliament was re-established as the supreme legislative institution, and the rights of the people against the sovereign power (including the right enshrined in *Habeas corpus*) were reaffirmed the following year in a Bill of Rights. So conceived, a right is a shield placed around the individual. And it is by reflecting on this concept that we will understand not only what is true in liberalism, but also the far-reaching disorders and falsehoods that have crept into politics under its aegis.

The idea that there are 'natural' or 'human' rights arose out of two distinct currents of opinion. There was the ancient belief in a universal code – the natural law – which applies to all people everywhere and which provides a standard against which any particular legal system can be measured. And there was the common-law assumption that law exists in part to protect the individual from arbitrary power. Combining those two ideas, Locke argued for a system of natural rights. These rights would guarantee that the individual is sovereign over his own life, able both to enter relations by agreement and to withdraw from them by mutual consent. On this understanding, incorporated in the 1689 Bill of Rights, human rights are to be understood as *liberties* – freedoms that we respect by leaving people alone. The doctrine of human rights is there to set limits to government, and cannot be used to authorize any increase in government power that is not required by the fundamental task of protecting individual liberty.

The original text of the European Convention on Human Rights also suggests that this is so; and the Convention spells out the implications of those rights – to life, liberty and the pursuit of happiness – advocated in the American Declaration of Independence. The Anglo-American tradition of constitutional thinking should be understood in this way, as addressing the question of how to limit the power of government, without losing its benefits. That tradition has given us the fixed points of liberal jurisprudence: the doctrine of the separation of powers, the theory of judicial independence, and the procedural idea of justice, according to which all citizens are equal before the law, and the judge must be impartial.

It is at this point, however, that the truth in liberalism slides almost unnoticeably into falsehood. For the search for liberty has gone hand in hand with a countervailing search for 'empowerment'. The negative freedoms offered by traditional theories of natural right, such as Locke's, do not compensate for the inequalities of power and opportunity in human societies. Hence egalitarians have begun to insert more positive rights into the list of negative freedoms, supplementing the liberty rights specified by the various international conventions with rights that do not merely demand non-encroachment from others, but which impose on them a positive duty. And in this they are drawing on the other root of the human rights idea – the root of 'natural law', which requires that every legal code conform to a universal standard.

This is apparent in the UN Declaration of Human Rights, which begins with a list of freedom rights and then suddenly, at Article 22, begins making radical claims against the state – claims that can be satisfied only by positive action from government. Here is Article 22:

> Everyone, as a member of society, has the right to social security and is entitled to realization, through national effort and international cooperation and in accordance with the organization and resources of each State, of the economic, social and cultural rights indispensable for his dignity and the free development of his personality.

There is a weight of political philosophy behind that article. Contained within this right is an unspecified list of other rights called 'economic, social and cultural', which are held to be indispensable not for freedom but for 'dignity' and the 'free development of personality'. Whatever this means in practice, it is quite clear that it is likely to involve a considerable extension of the field of human rights, beyond those basic liberties acknowledged in the American Declaration. Those basic liberties are arguably necessary for any kind of government by consent; the same is not true of the claims declared in Article 22 of the UN Declaration.

The Declaration goes on in this vein, conjuring a right to work, to leisure, to a standard of living sufficient to guarantee health – and other benefits which are, in effect, claims against the state rather than freedoms from its encroachments.

I don't say that those benefits are *not* rights: but even if they are rights, they are not justified in the same way as the freedom rights granted earlier in the Declaration. Moreover, they open the door to the 'rights inflation' that we have witnessed in recent decades, and to an interpretation of human rights that is prodigal of conflicts. When the 'right to a family life' declared by the European Convention of Human Rights enables a criminal who is also an illegal immigrant to escape deportation;[3] when the right to the traditional lifestyle of one's ethnic community, declared by the European Court of Human Rights, is used to install a park of mobile homes in defiance of planning law, so destroying property values all around;[4] when the Court of British Columbia discovers a 'right not to be offended' violated by a stand-up comedian's response to a lesbian couple ostentatiously snogging in the front row of his show;[5] when bankers claim their outrageous bonuses as a 'human right';[6] when the courts are burdened with these and similar cases, coming in at the rate of seven a day in Britain and at a cost of £2 billion a year to the taxpayer, we are entitled to ask whether the concept of a human right is after all securely founded, and whether there is any solid argument that would enable us to distinguish the true from the false among the many contenders.

The first point to note in response is that, as Dworkin puts it, 'rights are trumps'.[7] That is, in a court of law, if you can show that your interest in the

---

[3] *Mail online*, 6 December 2013 (accessed 1 February 2014).
[4] See below.
[5] *National Review online*, 21 April 2011 (accessed 1 February 2014).
[6] *Financial Times*, 7 October 2013.
[7] Ronald Dworkin, 'Taking Rights Seriously', in *Taking Rights Seriously* (Oxford: Oxford University Press, 1977).

matter is also protected as a right, then you win the case against anyone whose interests, however great, are not so protected. (Rights provide 'exclusionary reasons', in Raz's plausible way of putting it.)[8]

The second important point is that, unlike the solutions issued by a legislature, those issued by a court are not compromises: they are not attempts to reconcile the many interests involved in a situation, and the court does not see itself as formulating a policy for the good government of a community – that is the task of a legislature, not a court. The court sees itself as resolving a conflict in favour of one of the parties. In normal circumstances, a dispute over rights is a zero-sum game, in which one party wins everything, and the other loses everything. There are no consolation prizes. Moreover, the doctrine of precedent ensures that the court's decision will punch a hole in any legislation designed to solve issues of the kind that come before it. And this is one of the dangers inherent in 'human rights' legislation – namely, that it places in the hands of the ordinary citizen a tool with which even the most vital piece of public policy can be overturned in favour of the individual, regardless of the common interest and the common good. Thus terrorists in Britain have been able to overthrow attempts to deport them by claiming that this or that 'human right' would be violated by doing so. Without a criterion enabling us to distinguish genuine human rights from the many impostors we will never be sure that our legal provisions, however wise, benevolent and responsible, will be secure against the individual desire to escape from them.

The third important point is that the human rights declared by the various pieces of legislation, and the various decisions of the courts, are not obviously of the same philosophical, moral or political standing. A doctrine of human rights is entitled to the name only if the rights declared under it can be established *a priori*, in other words, as rights justified by philosophical reasoning rather than by the workings of a specific system of law. The attempt to do this, in the case of basic freedom rights, has been made by various writers – by Nozick, beginning from Kantian premises; by Finnis, beginning from Thomist premises; and so on.[9] I think we can all see the force of the idea that there are certain things that cannot be done to human beings – certain basic goods, including life itself,

---

[8]   Joseph Raz, *The Authority of Law* (Oxford: Oxford University Press, 1979).

[9]   Robert Nozick, *Anarchy, State and Utopia* (Cambridge, MA: Harvard University Press, 1974); John Finnis, *Natural Law and Natural Rights* (Oxford: Oxford University Press, 1980).

that cannot be taken away from them unless they in some way *forfeit* them. Life, limb and the basic freedom to pursue our goals undisturbed (compatible with a similar freedom enjoyed by others) are plausible candidates. You can see how the entitlement to these things lies at the heart of political cooperation: for without some guarantee that, in these respects at least, people are protected from invasion, there really could not be a system of law that enjoyed the free consent of those subject to it.[10]

Furthermore, we can understand those basic freedoms as rights partly because we can understand the reciprocal duty to respect them. My right to life is your duty not to kill me: and duties of non-encroachment and non-infliction are naturally upheld by morality and easily enforced by the law. However, once we step outside this narrowly circumscribed area of basic freedoms, we enter a much more shady and conflicted territory. The case in which a park of mobile homes was allowed to destroy the amenities of a settled village depended upon the provision for 'non-discrimination' – a provision that steps outside the area of basic freedoms, into that of justice.[11] And the striking thing is that this provision, meant to prevent one group of citizens from arbitrarily enjoying privileges denied to another, has been used precisely to claim for the minority privileges that are legally denied to the majority – the minority in this case being those who could claim to be 'travellers', apparently entitled to consideration as an 'ethnic group'.[12] Similar paradoxical consequences have emerged from the advocacy in America of 'positive discrimination', by which is meant a policy of giving to members of some once disadvantaged group legal privileges designed to 'rectify' their position.

The original purpose behind liberalism's invocation of natural rights was to protect the individual from arbitrary power. You held your rights, according to Locke and his followers, as an individual, and regardless of what group or class you belonged to. These rights force people to treat you as a free being, with sovereignty over your life, and as one who has an equal claim on others' respect. But the new ideas of human rights allow rights to one group that they deny to another: you have rights as the member of some ethnic minority or social class that cannot be claimed by every citizen. People can now be favoured

---

[10] This idea is beautifully built into his version of the social contract by Kant. See my *Kant: A Very Short Introduction* (Oxford: Oxford University Press, 2007), Chapter 7.

[11] Details in *Daily Mail online*, 8 October 2008 (accessed 1 February 2014).

[12] Race Relations Act 1976, and Human Rights Act 1998.

or condemned on account of their class, race, rank or occupation, and this in the name of liberal values. The rights that form the substance of international declarations therefore reflect a profound shift in liberal philosophy. The rhetoric of rights has shifted from freedoms to claims, and from equal treatment to equal outcomes.

A freedom right imposes a general duty on others to observe it; but it may arise from no specific relationship, and may make no specific demands of any individual. It is a right that may be invaded by others; but by doing nothing they respect it, and the duty to observe it is neither onerous nor a special responsibility of any particular person. Such is my right to move freely from place to place, my right to life, limb and property, and the other rights traditionally acknowledged as flowing from the natural law. You respect them by non-invasion, and the duty to respect them falls clearly and unambiguously on everyone.

That is not obviously the case with claims, especially when the claims are to non-specific benefits like health, education, a certain standard of living and so on. There are indeed elementary claims of morality, which impose an individual duty on the rest of us. It is reasonable to argue that the man set upon by thieves in Christ's famous parable had a claim – a moral claim – upon those who passed him by, and one that only the Good Samaritan was prepared to answer. But such cases of basic morality impose claims on each of us individually, and cannot be answered on our behalf by the state. As for the more specific claims that people make against each other – for succor, for a share of goods, for compensation – these demand a *history,* an account of the special relation between the claimant and the one against whom the claim arises, which will justify imposing this claim as a duty. In the absence of such a history, specifying who is liable to answer them, universal claims inevitably point to the state as the only possible provider. And large, vague claims require a massive expansion of state power, a surrender to the state of all kinds of responsibilities that previously vested in individuals, and the centralization of social life in the government machine. In other words, claim rights push us inevitably in a direction that, for many people, is not only economically disastrous, but morally unacceptable. It is a direction that is diametrically opposed to that for which the idea of a human right was originally introduced – a direction involving the increase, rather than the limitation, of the power of the state.

There is a deeper reason for disquiet over the extension of the natural right concept into the domain of claims. In an authoritative study, the American jurist Wesley Newcomb Hohfeld argued that the concept of a right belongs in a family of concepts – liability, immunity, duty, permission, power and so on – which are like modal concepts, such as possibility, necessity and probability, in identifying interlocking operations of rational thought.[13] The concept of a right belongs to a 'circle of juridical terms', which are intricately interdefinable, and which between them specify a systematic operation of the rational intellect. There is, as I would prefer to put it, a 'calculus of rights and duties', which rational beings use in order to settle their disputes and to reach agreement over matters of common or conflicting interest. The availability of this calculus is one of the things that distinguish us from the lower animals, and it would be available to us even if we did not attempt to back it up with a shared legal system. The concept of justice belongs to this calculus: injustice residing in the denial of rights or deserts, justice in 'giving to each his due', as the Roman Law (following Aristotle) expresses it.

Why do human beings make use of these juridical terms? What do they gain from it, and why has it stabilized in so many different parts of the world, so as to be received as entirely natural? The answer is that talk of rights has the function of enabling people to claim a sphere of personal sovereignty in which their choice is law. If I have a right to sit in a certain room then you cannot expel me from it without wronging me. By determining such rights we define the fixed points, the places of security, from which people can negotiate and agree. Without those fixed points, negotiation and free agreement are unlikely to occur, and if they occur, their outcome is unlikely to be stable. If I have no rights, then the agreement between us provides no guarantee of performance; my sphere of action is liable to constant invasion by others, and there is nothing that I can do to define the position from which I am negotiating in a way that compels you to acknowledge it.

Rights, then, enable us to establish a society in which consensual relations are the norm, and they do this by defining for each of us the sphere of sovereignty from which others are excluded. This explains Dworkin's view, in *Taking Rights Seriously*, that 'rights are trumps'. A right belongs to the fence that defines my sovereign territory: by claiming it, I put an absolute veto on things that you might do. It also explains the direct connection between right and duty: the

---

[13] W. N. Hohfeld, *Fundamental Legal Conceptions as Applied in Judicial Reasoning and Other Legal Essays* (New Haven, CT: Yale University Press, 1946); the original article appeared in the *Yale Law Journal*, 1917.

absoluteness of the right is tantamount to a duty to respect it. And it explains the zero-sum nature of disputes in a court of law, when rights are invoked to decide them.

If we look at rights in this way, as instruments that safeguard sovereignty, and so make free dealings between sovereign partners into the cement of society, then we see immediately why freedom rights have the best claim to universality, and why claim rights – detached from the moral law and from any specific history of responsibility and agreement – present a threat to the consensual order. A claim against another, if expressed as a right, is an imposition of a duty. If this duty arises from no free action or chain of responsibility that would provide a cogent ground for the claim, then by expressing it as a right we override the other's sovereignty. We say to him: here is something you must do or provide, even though your duty to do so arises from nothing you have done or for which you are responsible, and even though it is not a duty that follows from the moral law. This is simply a demand that you must satisfy.

How different such a case is, at least, from that of freedom rights. For these are by their very nature 'sovereignty protecting' devices. They are vetoes on what others can do to me or take from me, rather than demands that they do something or give something that I have an interest in their doing or giving. The duty that they define is one of non-interference, and the interest that they protect is the most fundamental interest that I have, namely my interest in retaining the power to make decisions for myself in those matters that most closely concern me.

It is evident from my discussion that the concepts of natural law and natural right raise the question of the relation between law and morality. Does the phrase 'natural law' simply refer to the constraints placed upon our conduct by moral judgement? If so should the legal system strive to give force to moral principles? Or does 'natural law' refer to some other constraint, more in keeping with the idea of a liberal society, in which different lifestyles and different 'conceptions of the good' can contend peacefully for their place in the sun? The history of 'Bills of Rights' since Locke suggests the latter conception: rights exist to protect and enlarge the space of moral choice, not to narrow it in accordance with some inquisitorial agenda.

In this spirit, John Stuart Mill argued forcefully that, whatever our moral principles, we will live together peacefully, respecting each other's freedom, only if we accept that our principles are not, as such, enforceable as law.[14] The state can restrict the liberty of the citizen, but only in order to protect his fellow citizens from harm. On this view, moral disapproval of an action is never sufficient to justify forbidding it by law. Mill's argument was successfully used in the 1960s to remove some of the more oppressive prohibitions on sexual conduct from English law. But nobody has been able to define 'harm' with the clarity that Mill's criterion requires. Subsequent statutes passed by the British Parliament have referred to 'public morality' as sufficient reason for criminalizing some activity, regardless of any proof of harm. (It is on these grounds that Parliament banned first fur farming, and then hunting with hounds.) And most people would not want to wait for proof of harm before criminalizing paedophilia. Clearly we are in difficult territory, where the temptation is to argue that others have no right to impose their morality on me, a free being, even though I have a perfect right to stop them doing the things that I find offensive.

In short, the relation between law and morality is deep and conflicted. But when it comes to the many claims made in the declarations of human rights, morality is doing all the work, with no constraint from practical politics or from the many conflicting interests that politicians must broker. The morality in question is not the old, conservative morality, based on family values and social respectability, but the morality of our urban elites, in which non-discrimination and the free choice of lifestyles take precedence over the old forms of social order.

Christ's parable of the Good Samaritan imposes a huge moral burden on us all. But to transfer this moral burden to the state, to say that it is for the state to transform that moral duty into a right of the recipient, and a right, moreover, against the state and therefore against society as a whole, is to take a large step away from the original liberal idea, of a state founded on the sovereignty of the individual. It is to move towards the new idea of a society ordered by an overarching morality, which may have little or nothing to do with the way people live. Judges in human rights courts therefore play with an abstract calculus of legal privileges, while passing the cost of their judgements to others with whom they have no connection. And nobody knows whether that cost can really be borne. It is this fact that is giving rise in Britain to a growing discontent

[14] *On Liberty.*

with human rights, and especially with the decisions of the foreign court tasked with inventing and imposing them.

At the same time, instead of limiting the power of the state, alleged human rights have begun to enhance that power, and to bring the state into all our disputes on the side of the favoured party. Rights, which for the liberal are the *sine qua non* of peaceful politics, become thereby a declaration of war on the majority culture.

7

The Truth in Multiculturalism

Conservatism as a political philosophy came into being with the Enlightenment. It would not have been possible without the scientific revolution, the overcoming of religious conflict, the rise of the secular state, and the triumph of liberal individualism. Conservatives for the most part acknowledged the benefits contained in the new conception of citizenship, which vested power in the people, and in the state as their appointed – and in part elected – representative. They also recognized the great reversal in the affairs of government that this implied. Henceforth, they saw, accountability is from the top down, and not from the bottom up. The rulers must answer to the ruled, and responsibilities at every level are no longer imposed but assumed.

At the same time, conservatives sounded a warning against the Enlightenment. For Herder, Maistre, Burke and others, the Enlightenment was not to be regarded as a complete break with the past. It made sense only against the background of a long-standing cultural inheritance. Liberal individualism offered a new and in many ways inspiring vision of the human condition; but it depended upon traditions and institutions that bound people together in ways that no merely individualistic worldview could engender. The Enlightenment proposed a universal human nature, governed by a universal moral law, from which the state emerges through the consent of the governed. The political process was henceforth to be shaped by the free choices of individuals, in order to protect the institutions that make free choices possible. It was all beautiful and logical and inspiring. But it made no sense without the cultural inheritance of the nation state, and the forms of social life that had taken root in it.

In this connection, Herder famously distinguished *Kultur* from *Zivilisation*, arguing that, while the second could be shared between the nations of Europe – and indeed increasingly was shared – the first was distinctive of each of them. Maistre, reacting against the French Revolution and the idolatrous idea, as he saw it, of the Nation as the fount of all law and the object of all worship, pointed towards the Christian heritage, and the God-made character of both the primary social institutions (marriage and the family) and the constitutions that establish political order. Burke argued that custom, tradition and 'prejudice' are the preconditions of political order, that they contain wisdom that could never be put together by the deliberations of rational individuals, and that without them society would disintegrate into the 'dust and powder of individuality'.

All such thoughts were issued as warnings. The freedom won through enlightenment, they implied, was a fragile and threatened thing. It depended upon a cultural base that it could not itself guarantee. Only if people are held together by stronger bonds than the bond of free choice can free choice be raised to the prominence that the new political order promised. And those stronger bonds are buried deep in the community, woven by custom, ceremony, language and religious need. Political order, in short, requires cultural unity, something that politics itself can never provide.

That sceptical note sounded throughout the nineteenth century, in answer to the growing spirit of democratic government. But its impact was gradually softened, as politics became part of the culture. In the English-speaking world especially, people began to appreciate that culture is not the atavistic and buried thing that Herder invoked, residing in ancient custom, spiritual intimations and the language of the folk. Culture is permeable to the rest of social life, adapts to institutions, which in turn adapt to the emancipation of the people. Wasn't the Glorious Revolution of 1688 a proof of this, with its rearrangement of the place of religion in the life of the *polis*? Wasn't the American Revolution also such a proof, bringing the political thought of the Enlightenment into the centre of social life, and achieving an astonishing, nationwide agreement concerning the role of the state and the rights of the individual in the face of it? The entire culture of America was changed by this, and it is fair to say that, in the American case, the world encountered a nation created by politics. The new nation identified itself explicitly as 'the land of the free', and it had even insisted, in the first amendment to the Constitution, that freedom of religion is the first right of the citizen, and an absolute barrier to the powers of Congress.

It is notorious that there were, and are, clashes between the civil order imposed by the Constitution and the local attachments of the American communities – one of them leading to a devastating civil war. Nevertheless, over time, there emerged in America, and throughout the English-speaking world, what one might call a 'civic culture' – a sense of the political process as consonant with national attachment, as arising from and endorsing the place, the way of life and the inheritance of institutions and laws, to which the citizen is by destiny attached. In this way the Enlightenment idea of citizenship has been wound into the underlying loyalty of the people.

And this, I maintain, is the truth in multiculturalism. Thanks to the 'civic culture' that has grown in the post-Enlightenment West, social membership has been freed from religious affiliation, from racial, ethnic and kinship ties, and from the 'rites of passage' whereby communities lay claim to the souls of their members, by guarding them against the pollution of other customs and other tribes. It is why it is so easy to emigrate to Western states – nothing more is required of the immigrant than the adoption of the civic culture, and the assumption of the duties implied in it.

It does not follow that political obligation is reduced to a contract, even if there are people who treat it in that way. It is still rooted in a defined pre-political membership, in which territory, history, neighbourhood and custom play a decisive role. But this pre-political membership has proved permeable to the liberal individualist view of the citizen. Our obligations to others, to the country and to the state have been revised in a direction that has opened the way to the admission of people from outside the community – provided that they, too, can live according to the liberal ideal of citizenship. Needless to say many immigrants come to Western countries – and to the English-speaking countries especially – in search of the advantages that liberal jurisdiction brings, and without understanding or accepting the costs. And many become disaffected with a form of loyalty that is so seemingly abstruse, detached and purged of the warm togetherness of religion. But that is another matter, and one to which I return.

The Enlightenment vision of human nature was based on the idea that human beings everywhere enjoy the same reasoning powers, and that these powers lead of their own accord towards a common morality and a common repertoire of passions. Works of art from the European Enlightenment took as their subject matter other cultures, other countries and other climes, so as expressly to profile the shared humanity of the different peoples of the world. Examples like Montesquieu's *Lettres Persanes*, Lessing's *Nathan der Weise*, Mozart's *Die Entführung aus dem Serail*, MacPherson's Ossian poems, Goethe's *Westöstlicher Diwan*, and a thousand lesser creations remind us of the immense curiosity that grew in European and American society, towards the varieties of human experience and community. And it is thanks to the work of Western anthropologists in the nineteenth century that we know so much about the way human beings are, before technology, science and the knowledge of modern life impinge upon them.

The long-term effect of this has been to open Western societies to immigration, and to impart an ideal of citizenship that, it is hoped, will enable people of disparate origins and backgrounds to live together, recognizing that the real source of their obligations lies not in that which divides them – race and religion in particular – but in that which unites them – territory, good government, the day-to-day routines of neighbourliness, the institutions of civil society, and the workings of the law. Sometimes it works, sometimes it doesn't. And that is what we must expect. And if it is to work it will be thanks to the effort on both sides to integrate the new arrivals into the surrounding way of life, so that the common culture of citizenship adapts to include them.

Such is the truth in multiculturalism. As a result of the Enlightenment and all that it has meant for Western civilization, communities can be absorbed and integrated into our way of life, even when they arrive bearing strange gods. But this virtue of our civilization, so clearly manifest in America, has been used precisely to repudiate that civilization's claim on us, to argue, in the name of multiculturalism, that we need to marginalize our inherited customs and beliefs, even to cast them off, in order to become an 'inclusive' society in which all our newcomers feel at home, regardless of any effort to adapt to their new surroundings. This has been urged on us in the name of political correctness, which has gone hand in hand with the kind of repudiating liberalism that I described at the end of the previous chapter.

Political correctness exhorts us to be as 'inclusive' as we can, to discriminate neither in thought, word nor deed against ethnic, sexual, religious or behavioural minorities. And in order to be inclusive we are encouraged to denigrate what is felt to be most especially *ours*. The Director-General of the BBC recently condemned his organization and its programmes as obnoxiously white and middle-class. Academics sneer at the curriculum established by 'Dead White European Males'. A British race-relations charity has condemned the affirmation of a 'British' national identity as racist. All such abusive utterances express the code of political correctness. For although they involve the deliberate condemnation of people on grounds of class, race, sex or colour, the purpose is not to exclude the Other but to condemn Ourselves. The gentle advocacy of inclusion masks the far from gentle desire to exclude the old excluder: in other words, to repudiate the cultural inheritance that defines us.

The 'down with us' mentality is devoted to rooting out old and unsustainable loyalties. And when the old loyalties die, so does the old form of membership. Enlightenment, which seems to lead of its own accord to a culture of repudiation, thereby destroys enlightenment, by undermining the certainties on which citizenship is founded. This is what we have witnessed in the intellectual life of the West.

The most interesting aspect of this culture of repudiation has been the attack on the central place accorded to reason in human affairs by the writers, philosophers and political theorists of the Enlightenment. The old appeal to reason is seen merely as an appeal to Western values, which have made reason into a shibboleth, and thereby laid claim to an objectivity that no culture could possibly possess. For cultures offer membership, not truth, and can therefore make no exclusive claims on the one who sees them from a point of view outside their territory. Moreover, by claiming reason as its source, Western culture has (according to the 'post-modernist' critique) concealed its ethno-centrism; it has dressed up Western ways of thinking as though they have universal force. Reason, therefore, is a lie, and by exposing the lie we reveal the oppression at the heart of our culture.

The dethroning of reason goes hand in hand with a disbelief in objective truth. The authorities whose works are most often cited in debunking 'Western culture' are all hardened disbelievers. No argument can be wielded in the face of their contempt for the culture that makes argument possible. As the sceptic quickly discovers, the laws of truth and rational deduction are impossible to defend without at the same time presupposing them. A kind of meta-logical impasse confronts the defenders of the old curriculum and the discipline expressed in it, and they watch in silence as the new anti-authoritarian authorities colonize their patch.

Nietzsche is a favourite, since he made the point explicitly: 'There are no truths,' he wrote, 'only interpretations.' Either what Nietzsche said is true – in which case it is not true, since there are no truths – or it is false. But it is only from the standpoint of the Enlightenment that this response seems like a refutation. The new curriculum is in the business of marginalizing refutation, just as it marginalizes truth. This explains the appeal of those recent thinkers – Michel Foucault, Jacques Derrida and Richard Rorty – who owe their intellectual eminence not to their arguments but to their role in giving authority to the rejection of authority, and to their absolute commitment to the impossibility of absolute commitments. In each of them you find the view that truth, objectivity, value or meaning are chimerical, and that all we can have, and all we need to have, is the warm security of our own opinion.[1] Hence it is in vain to argue against the new authorities. No argument, however rational, can counter the massive 'will to believe' that captures their normal readers. After all, a rational argument assumes precisely what they 'put in question' – namely, the possibility of rational argument. Each of them owes his reputation to a kind of religious faith: faith in the relativity of all opinions, including this one. For this is the faith on which a new form of membership is founded – a first-person plural of denial.

This can be witnessed very clearly in the writings of Richard Rorty, who advocates what is in effect a retreat from the Enlightenment idea of reason in the name of something he calls 'pragmatism', assuming himself to stand in the tradition established by C. S. Peirce and William James, according to whom the scientific truth of a belief and its practical usefulness are not independent virtues. The most useful belief is the one that gives the best handle on the world: the belief which, when acted upon, holds out the greatest prospect of success. Obviously, however, that is not a sufficient characterization of the difference between the true and the false. Anyone seeking a career in an American university will find feminist beliefs useful, just as racist beliefs were useful to the university apparatchik in Nazi Germany. But this hardly shows those beliefs to be true. So what do we *really* mean by 'useful'? One suggestion is this: a belief is useful when it is part of a successful theory. But a successful theory is one that makes true predictions. Hence we have gone round in a circle, defining truth by utility and utility by truth. Indeed, it is hard to find a plausible pragmatism that does not come down to this: that a true proposition is one that is useful in the way that *true* propositions are useful. Impeccable, but vacuous.

The threat of vacuity does not deter Rorty, who sees pragmatism as a weapon against the old idea of reason. Even though he fails dismally to say what pragmatism really consists in, this failure is of no interest to his followers, who take it in their stride. For Rorty invokes his pragmatism as a kind of magic spell which, once cast, takes us into a world where the writ of reason does not run. It is this that qualifies him for guru status in departments of humanities. In his words:

[1] I have tried to present the case against Foucault and Derrida in *An Intelligent Person's Guide to Modern Culture* (South Bend, IN: St Augustine's Press, 2000); reissued as *Modern Culture* (London: Continuum, 2004).

> Pragmatists view truth as ... what is good for *us* to believe ... They see the gap between truth and justification not as something to be bridged by isolating a natural and trans-cultural sort of rationality which can be used to criticise certain cultures and praise others, but simply as the gap between the actual good and the possible better ... For pragmatists, the desire for objectivity is not the desire to escape the limitations of one's community, but simply the desire for as much intersubjective agreement as possible, the desire to extend the reference of 'us' as far as we can.[2]

In other words, pragmatism enables us to dismiss the idea of a 'trans-cultural ... rationality'. There is no point to the old ideas of objectivity and universal truth; all that matters is the fact that *we* agree.

But who are we? And what do we agree about? Turn to Rorty's essays, and you will soon find out. 'We' are all feminists, liberals, advocates of gay liber-ation and the open curriculum; 'we' do not believe in God, or in any inherited religion; nor do the old ideas of authority, order and self-discipline carry weight for us. 'We' make up our minds as to the meaning of texts by creating through our words the consensus that includes us. There is no constraint on us, beyond the community to which we have chosen to belong. And because there is no objective truth but only our own self-engendered consensus, our position is unassailable from any point of view outside it. The pragmatist may not only decide what to think; he can protect himself from whoever doesn't think the same.

A true pragmatist will no doubt invent history just as he invents everything else, by persuading 'us' to agree with him. Nevertheless, it is worth taking a glance at history, if only to see how paradoxical and dangerous is Rorty's view of the human intellect. The Islamic *ummah* – the society of all believers – was and remains the most extended consensus of opinion that the world has ever known. It expressly recognizes consensus (*ijma'*), as a criterion of religious truth, and is engaged in a never-ceasing endeavour to include as many as possible in its comprehensive first-person plural. Moreover, whatever Rorty means by 'good' or 'better' beliefs, the pious Muslim must surely count as having some of the very best: beliefs that bring security, stability, happiness, a handle on the world, and a cheerful conscience in opposition to the *kāfiroun* who think otherwise. Yet still, is there not a nagging feeling somewhere, that those heart-warming

---

[2] Richard Rorty, *Objectivity, Realism and Truth* (Cambridge: Cambridge University Press), pp. 22–3.

beliefs might not be true, and that the enervated opinions of the post-modern atheist might just have the edge on them? In Rorty's account of pragmatism, this is not something that a pragmatist can say, even though it is something that Rorty believes.

All such attempts to slide out of the obligations that reason imposes on us involve a kind of repudiation of the Western Enlightenment. In its own eyes, the Enlightenment was not the narrow and provincial thing that Rorty imagines himself to be condemning. It involved the celebration of universal values and a common human nature. The art of the Enlightenment ranged over other places, other times and other cultures, in a heroic attempt to vindicate a vision of humanity as free and self-created. That vision inspired and was inspired by the old curriculum, the very curriculum that Rorty wished to put in question.

This explains the popularity of another relativist thinker – Edward Saïd – whose book *Orientalism* showed how to dismiss the Enlightenment as a form of cultural imperialism.[3] The Orient appears in Western art and literature, Saïd argues, as something exotic, unreal, theatrical, and therefore unfounded. Far from being a generous acknowledgement of other cultures, the Orientalist art of Enlightenment Europe (Lessing's *Nathan der weise*, for instance, or Goethe's *Westöstlicher Diwan*) is a screen behind which those cultures are concealed. The Orient might have been a genuine alternative to the Western Enlightenment; instead, it is remade as a decorative foil to the Western imperial project.

In this view, the old Enlightenment curriculum is really mono-cultural, devoted to perpetuating the view of Western civilization as inherently superior to its rivals. Its assumption of a universal rational perspective, from the vantage point of which all humanity could be studied, is nothing better than a rationalization of its imperialist claims. By contrast, we who live in the amorphous and multicultural environment of the post-modern city must open our hearts and minds to all cultures, and be wedded to none. The inescapable result of this is relativism: the recognition that no culture has any special claim to our attention, and that no culture can be judged or dismissed from outside.

But once again there is a paradox. For those who advocate this multicultural approach are as a rule vehement in their dismissal of Western culture. While exhorting us to judge other cultures on their own terms, Saïd is also asking us to judge Western culture from an external perspective – to set it against alternatives, and to judge it adversely, as ethnocentric and even racist.

---

[3]   Edward Saïd, *Orientalism* (New York: Pantheon, 1978).

Furthermore, the criticisms offered of Western culture are really confir-
mations of its claim to favour. It is thanks to the Enlightenment, and its
universalist morality, that racial and sexual equality have such a common-
sense appeal to us. It is the Enlightenment conception of man that makes
us demand so much of Western art and literature – more than we should
ever demand of the art and literature of Java, Borneo or China. It is the very
attempt to embrace other cultures that makes Western art a hostage to Saïd's
strictures – an attempt that has no real parallel in the traditional art of Arabia,
India or Africa. Of course, influences have passed both ways in the many
encounters between West and East. The Arabic exponents of *Falāsifa* learned
what they could from Greek philosophy, and passed their learning to their
Christian neighbours in Andalusia. And in those fertile years of interaction it
would have been hard to say which civilization was the tutor and which the
pupil in the matters that passed between them. Nevertheless, the particular
vector of thinking, which has sent artists, poets, musicians and philosophers
on self-conscious journeys of discovery into other cultures, other places and
other times, has no real equivalent outside the Enlightenment. One instance
of this, indeed, is the tradition of Oriental scholarship that arose during
the eighteenth century and which produced such extraordinary exponents
of other cultures as Sir William Jones of Calcutta and Max Müller, without
whose work the classical literature of India would be virtually unknown
today.[4]

Moreover, it is only a very narrow view of our artistic tradition that does not
discover in it a multicultural approach that is far more imaginative than anything
that is now taught under that name. Well before the Enlightenment, Western
culture was in the habit of celebrating universal human values. While rooted
in the Christian experience, it has drawn from that source a wealth of human
feeling that it spreads impartially over imagined worlds. From *Orlando Furioso*
and *Don Quixote* to Byron's *Don Juan*, from Monteverdi's *L'Incoronazione di
Poppeia* to Longfellow's *Hiawatha*, from *The Winter's Tale* to *Madama Butterfly*
and *Das Lied von der Erde*, Western culture has continuously ventured into
spiritual territory that has no place on the Christian map. Those great aesthetic
achievements belong with the secular rule of law, territorial jurisdiction and the

---

[4] The story is told, in part, by Robert Irwin, in *Dangerous Knowledge: Orientalism
and its Discontents* (Woodstock, NY: Overlook Press, 2006). Irwin mounts a
crushing refutation of Saïd.

aspiration towards citizenship, as products of the loyalties that enable men and women to identify in imagination with those from 'elsewhere'.

The culture of repudiation marks a crumbling of the Enlightenment in other ways. As is frequently remarked, the spirit of free enquiry is now disappearing from schools and universities in the West. Books are put on or struck off the curriculum on grounds of political correctness; speech codes and counselling services police the language and conduct of both students and teachers; many courses are designed to impart ideological conformity rather than free enquiry, and students are often penalized for having drawn some heretical conclusion about the leading issues of the day. In sensitive areas, such as the study of race and sex, censorship is overtly directed not only at students but also at any teacher, however impartial and scrupulous, who comes up with the wrong conclusions.

The culture of repudiation therefore reminds us that free enquiry is not a normal exercise of the human mind, and is attractive only when seen as an avenue to membership. When the experience of membership can no longer be obtained in such a way, a new kind of enquiry takes over, one explicitly directed towards a promised social goal and a substitute for the old and rejected forms of attachment. A single theme runs through the humanities as they are regularly taught in American and European universities, which is that of the illegitimacy of Western civilization, and of the artificial nature of the distinctions on which it has been based. All distinctions are 'cultural', therefore 'constructed', therefore 'ideological', in the sense defined by Marx – manufactured by the ruling groups or classes in order to serve their interests and bolster their power. Western civilization is simply the record of that oppressive process, and the principal purpose of studying it is to deconstruct its claim to our membership. This is the core belief that a great many students in the humanities are required to ingest, preferably before they have the intellectual discipline to question it, or to set it against the literature that shows it to be untenable.

To put the point in another way, the Enlightenment displaced theology from the heart of the curriculum, in order to put the disinterested pursuit of truth in place of it. Within a very short time, however, we find the university dominated by theology of another kind – a godless theology, to be sure, but one no less insistent upon unquestioning submission to doctrine, and no less ardent in its pursuit of heretics, sceptics and debunkers. People are no longer burned at the stake for their views: they simply fail to get tenure, or, if they are students, they flunk the course. But the effect is similar, namely to reinforce an orthodoxy in which nobody really believes.

Aristotle told us that all human beings desire to know; but he failed to point out that they do so only when first reassured that knowledge will be reassuring. People turn from uncomfortable truths, and construct walls that will hide them from view. It is difficult to construct such a wall on your own; but in partnership with others, and protected by a well-endowed institution, you can add your own block of adamantine prose to the ramparts. The purpose is not to tell lies, but to create an acceptable *public doctrine*. And a public doctrine is acceptable if it provides the foundation for a stable and internally secure human community. In short, the vast changes in the cultural life of Western societies have their origin in the search for community, among people for whom the old loyalties have lost their appeal.

In place of the old beliefs based on godliness, judgement and historical attachment, young people are given the new beliefs based on equality and inclusion, and are told that the judgement of other lifestyles is a crime. If the purpose were merely to substitute one belief system for another it would be open to rational debate. But the purpose is to substitute one *community* for another. The project, however, is a purely negative one – of severing young people from attachments that have lost their moral and religious dynamism. The 'non-judgemental' attitude to other cultures goes hand in hand with a fierce denunciation of the culture that might have been one's own – something that we have witnessed repeatedly in the American opinion-forming elites since 11 September 2001. Unfortunately, however, there is no such thing as a community based in repudiation. The assault on the old cultural inheritance leads to no new form of membership, but only to a kind of alienation. It is for this reason, it seems to me, that we must be cultural conservatives. The alternative is the kind of nihilism that lurks just below the surface in the writings of Rorty, Saïd, Derrida and Foucault.

Perhaps the worst aspect of this nihilism is the routine accusation of 'racism', levelled against anyone who offers to endorse, to teach and to uphold the values of Western civilization. Fear of the charge of racism has led commentators, politicians and police forces all across the Western world to refrain from criticizing or taking action against many of the overtly criminal customs that have installed themselves in our midst – customs such as forced marriage, female circumcision and 'honour' killing, and the growing intimidation from Islamists of anyone remotely critical of their faith.

The charge of 'racism' represents an attempt to turn the culture of repudiation in a religious direction – to make the posture of not belonging into a new kind of belonging, with enemies, banners and an onward march to victory over the status quo. But it depends upon a deep untruth – the untruth that race and culture are the same thing, whereas in fact they have nothing to do with each other. There is no contradiction in the idea that Felix Mendelssohn was Jewish by race and German by culture – or indeed that he was the most public-spirited representative of German culture in his day. Nor is there any contradiction in saying that a single person belongs to two cultures. Felix's grandfather Moses was a great rabbi, upstanding representative of the Jewish cultural inheritance and also founding father of the German Enlightenment. Many of the German philologists to whom the Enlightenment gave rise were as multicultural as Moses Mendelssohn – Max Müller, for example, German by birth, English by adoption, and more steeped in the classical culture of India than virtually anyone alive today. Wagner had to twist and turn his thoughts into every kind of absurd contortion in order to discover 'Jewishness' in the music of Felix Mendelssohn, from whom he took so much. And Wagner's repugnant essay on Judaism in music is one of the first instances of the lie that we have had to live through – the lie that sees race and culture as the same idea, and which tells us that in demanding a measure of cultural uniformity, we are also affirming the dominance of a single race.

Once we distinguish race and culture, the way is open to acknowledge that not all cultures are equally admirable, and that not all cultures can exist comfortably side by side. To deny this is to forgo the very possibility of moral judgement, and therefore to deny the fundamental experience of community. It is precisely this that has caused the multiculturalists to hesitate. It is culture, not nature, that tells a family that their daughter who has fallen in love outside the permitted circle must be killed, that girls must undergo genital mutilation if they are to be respectable, that the infidel must be destroyed when Allah commands it. You can read about those things and think that they belong to the pre-history of our world. But when suddenly they are happening in your midst, you are apt to wake up to the truth about the culture that advocates them. You are apt to say, that is not *our* culture, and it has no business *here*. And you will probably be tempted to go one stage further, the stage that the Enlightenment naturally invites, and to say that it has no business anywhere.

For what is being brought home to us, through painful experiences that we might have avoided had it been permitted before now to say the truth, is that we, like everyone else, depend upon a shared culture for our security, our prosperity and our freedom to be. We don't require everyone to have the same faith, to lead the same kind of family life or to participate in the same festivals. But we have a shared civic culture, a shared language and a shared public sphere. Our societies are built upon the Judaeo-Christian ideal of neighbour-love, according to which strangers and intimates deserve equal concern. They require each of us to respect the freedom and sovereignty of every person, and to acknowledge the threshold of privacy beyond which it is a trespass to go unless invited. Our societies depend upon law-abidingness and open contracts, and they reinforce these things through the educational traditions that have shaped our common curriculum. It is not an arbitrary cultural imperialism that leads us to value Greek philosophy and literature, the Hebrew Bible, Roman law, and the medieval epics and romances and to teach these things in our schools. They are *ours*, in just the way that the legal order and the political institutions are ours: they form part of what made us, and convey the message that it is right to be what we are. And reason endorses these things, and tells us that our civic culture is not just a parochial possession of inward-looking communities, but a justified way of life.

Over time, immigrants can come to share these things with us: the experience of America bears ample witness to this. And they more easily do so when they recognize that, in any meaningful sense of the word, our culture is also a multi-culture, incorporating elements absorbed in ancient times from all around the Mediterranean basin and in modern times from the adventures of European traders and explorers across the world. But this kaleidoscopic culture is still *one* thing, with a set of inviolable principles at its core; and it is the source of social cohesion across Europe and America. Our culture allows for a great range of ways of life; it enables people to privatize their religion and their family customs, while still belonging to the public realm of open dealings and shared allegiance. For it defines that public realm in legal and territorial terms, and not in terms of creed or kinship.

So what happens when people whose identity is fixed by creed or kinship immigrate into places settled by Western culture? The activists say that we must make room for them, and that we do this by relinquishing the space in which *their* culture can flourish. Our political class has at last recognized that this is a recipe for disaster, and that we can welcome immigrants only if we welcome them *into* our culture, and not beside or against it. But that means telling them to accept rules, customs and procedures that may be alien to their old way of life. Is this an injustice? I do not think that it is. If immigrants come it is because they gain by doing so. It is therefore reasonable to remind them that there is also a cost. Only now, however, is our political class prepared to say so, and to insist that the cost be paid.

8

The Truth in Environmentalism

Conservatives endorse Burke's view of society, as a partnership between the living, the unborn and the dead; they believe in civil association between neighbours rather than intervention by the state; and they accept that the most important thing the living can do is to settle down, to make a home for themselves, and to pass that home to their children. *Oikophilia*, the love of home, lends itself to the environmental cause, and it is astonishing that the many conservative parties in the English-speaking world have not seized hold of that cause as their own.

There are two reasons for this, I believe. The first is that the conservative cause has been polluted by the ideology of big business, by the global ambitions of the multinational companies, and by the ascendancy of economics in the thinking of modern politicians. Those factors have led conservatives to enter into alliance with people who regard the effort to conserve things as both futile and quaint. The second reason is that the truth in environmentalism has been obscured by the agitated propaganda of the environmentalists and by the immensity of the problems that they put before us. When the attention of the world is directed towards global warming, climate change, mass extinctions and melting ice caps – all of which lie outside the reach of any national government, and for none of which does a remedy immediately present itself – the result is a loss of confidence in ordinary politics, a despair at human incapacity, and a last ditch adoption of radical internationalist schemes that involve a surrender of sovereignty.

In the next chapter I will say something about the truth in internationalism. But it is well to acknowledge at this juncture the great danger that it presents to the work of politics, in leveraging the transfer of power from elected and accountable politicians to unelected and unaccountable bureaucrats. Once this leverage has occurred, ordinary citizens are tempted to give up on the matter, and to bury their heads in the sand.

But the truth in environmentalism is one that is fundamental to the idea of political order, and one that has been acknowledged by the English common law throughout its history. Over a large range of cases, environmental problems arise from our entirely reasonable habit of taking the benefits of our activities, while passing on the costs. The environment is degraded because we externalize the costs of what we do; and the solution is to find the motives that will return the costs to the one who creates them.

There is a tendency among environmentalists to single out the big players in the market as the principal culprits: to pin environmental crime on those – like oil companies, motor manufacturers, logging corporations, agribusinesses, supermarkets – that make their profits by exporting their costs to others (including others who are not yet born). But this is to mistake the effect for the cause. In a free economy such ways of making money emerge by an invisible hand from choices made by all of us. It is the demand for cars, oil, cheap food and expendable luxuries that is the real cause of the industries that provide these things. Of course it is true that the big players externalize their costs whenever they can. But so do we. Whenever we travel by air, visit the supermarket, or consume fossil fuels, we are exporting our costs to others, and to future generations. A free economy is driven by individual demand. And in a free economy, individuals, just as much as big businesses, strive to export the cost of what they do.

The solution is not the socialist one, of abolishing the free economy, since this merely places massive economic power in the hands of unaccountable bureaucrats, who are equally in the business of exporting their costs, while enjoying secure rents on the social product. The solution is to adjust our demands, so as to bear the costs of them ourselves, and to find the way to put pressure on businesses to do likewise. And we can correct ourselves in this way only if we have motives to do so – motives strong enough to restrain our appetites.

Rational self-interest has an important part to play. But it is subject to the well-known paradoxes of social choice, which arise when self-interested agents combine in pursuit of resources that are affected by their decisions. To the well-known free rider and prisoner's dilemma problems, environmentalists have added 'the tragedy of the commons' – the situation that arises when people compete for their share of a finite resource and as a result exhaust it. Social contract theorists, from Hobbes to Rawls, have attempted to overcome the problems of social choice, but always they come up against some version of the original difficulty: why is it more reasonable to bide by the contract than to pretend to bide by it? Increasingly the response to these problems has been a bureaucratic one: to establish a system of regulations that create the incentives to conserve, rather than to deplete, the resources on which we collectively depend. But, as I try to show in *Green Philosophy*, this response, while often a necessary first step, creates negative incentives of its own, while lifting the problem from the hands of those best adapted to solving it.

The need is for non-egotistical motives that can be elicited in ordinary members of society, and relied upon to serve the long-term ecological goal. We should recognize that environmental protection is a lost cause if we cannot find the incentives that would lead people in general, and not merely their self-appointed and non-elected representatives, to advance it. Here is where environmentalists and conservatives can and should make common cause. That common cause is territory – the object of a love that has found its strongest political expression through the nation state.

Many environmentalists will acknowledge that local loyalties and local concerns must be given a proper place in our decision-making, if we are to counter the adverse effects of the global economy. Hence the oft-repeated slogan: 'Think globally, act locally.' However, they will tend to baulk at the suggestion that local loyalty should be seen in national terms, rather than as the small-scale expression of a humane universalism. Yet there is a very good reason for emphasizing nationality. For nations are communities with a political shape. They are predisposed to assert their sovereignty, by translating the common sentiment of belonging into collective decisions and self-imposed laws. Nationality is a form of territorial attachment, but it is also a proto-legislative arrangement. Moreover, nations are collective agents in the sphere of global decision-making. Through membership in a nation the individual has a voice in global affairs.

It is through developing this idea, of a territorial sentiment that contains the seeds of sovereignty within itself, that conservatives make their distinctive contribution to ecological thinking. Were conservatism to adopt a slogan, it should be 'Feel locally, think nationally.' In the current environmental crisis, there is no agent to take the needed measures, and no focus of loyalty to secure consent to them, other than the nation state. Rather than attempt to rectify environmental and social problems at the global level, therefore, conservatives seek a reassertion of local sovereignty over known and managed environments. This involves affirming the right of nations to self-government, and to the adoption of policies that will chime with local loyalties and customs. It also involves opposing the all-pervasive tendency of modern government towards centralization, and actively returning to local communities some of the powers confiscated by central bureaucracies – including those confiscated by transnational institutions like the World Trade Organization, the United Nations and the European Union.

Indeed, it is only at the local level that it is realistic to hope for improvement. For there is no evidence that global political institutions have done anything to limit the damage – on the contrary, by encouraging communication around the world, and by eroding national sovereignty and legislative barriers, they have fed into the global entropy and weakened the only true sources of resistance to it. I know many environmentalists who agree with me that the WTO and the World Bank are potential threats to the environment, not merely by breaking down self-sufficient and self-reproducing peasant economies, but also by eroding national sovereignty wherever this places an obstacle before the goal of free trade.[1] Many also seem to agree with me that traditional communities deserve protection from sudden and externally engineered change, not merely for the sake of their sustainable economies, but also because of the values and loyalties that constitute the sum of their social capital.

But we too deserve protection from global entropy, and we too must retain what we can of the loyalties that attach us to our territory, and make of that territory a home. Yet, in so far as we have seen any successful attempts to reverse the tide of ecological destruction, these have issued from national or local schemes to protect places recognized as 'ours' – defined, in other words, through some inherited entitlement. I think of the volunteers and campaigners who set out to protect the natural environment of Great Britain in the nineteenth century; the English National Trust, a civic association with four million members, dedicated to conserving our countryside and its settlements; the initiative of American nature lovers, acting upon the United States Congress, to create national parks; the action by Iceland to protect the breeding ground of the Atlantic cod; the legislation that freed Ireland from polythene bags; the clean energy initiatives in Sweden and Norway; the Swiss planning

---

[1] Criticisms of these institutions from the left are assembled on the websites of the Global Justice Center and the Global Justice Ecology Center. See also the informed scepticism expressed by Joseph Stiglitz, *Globalization and Its Discontents* (New York and London: W. W. Norton, 2002) and *Making Globalization Work* (New York and London: W. W. Norton, 2006).

laws that have enabled local communities to retain control over their environments and to manage those environments as a shared possession; the British 'Green Belt' policies that brought an end to urban sprawl; the initiatives of lobster-catchers in Maine and cod-fishers in Norway to establish self-regulating fisheries with local people in charge. Those are small-scale achievements, but they are real, and could, if replicated more widely, change the face of the earth for the better.[2] Moreover, they are successful because they appeal to a natural motive – the shared attachment to a shared place, and to the resources that it provides to those who live in it.

That, it seems to me, is the goal towards which serious environmentalism and serious conservatism both point – namely, home, the place where we are and that we share, the place that defines us, that we hold in trust for our descendants, and that we don't want to spoil. Nobody seems to have identified a motive more likely to serve the environmentalist cause than this one. It is a motive in ordinary people. It can provide a foundation both for a conservative approach to institutions and a conservationist approach to the land. It is a motive that might permit us to reconcile the demand for democratic participation with the respect for future generations and the duty of trusteeship. It is, in my view, the only serious resource that we have, in our fight to maintain local order in the face of globally stimulated decay.

Self-styled conservatives have been much criticized – often rightly – for their belief that all political decisions are really economic decisions, and that market solutions are the only solutions there are. But, as I suggested in Chapter 2, we must put the *oikos* back into *oikonomia*. Respect for the *oikos* is the real reason why conservatives dissociate themselves from currently fashionable forms of environmental activism. Radical environmentalists tend to define their goals in global and international terms, and support NGOs and pressure groups that will fight the multinational predators on their own territory and with weapons that make no use of national sovereignty. But, as I try to show in detail in *Green Philosophy*, their arguments go nowhere, precisely because they identify no motive that will animate ordinary passive people, without whose cooperation no solution is viable.

[2] Some of these consensual solutions have been the subject of an important study by Elinor Ostrom. I engage with her arguments in Chapter 5 of *Green Philosophy*. Some have also been documented in Chapter 5 of William A. Shutkin, *The Land that Could Be: Environmentalism and Democracy in the Twenty-First Century* (Cambridge, MA: MIT Press, 2001).

The truth in environmentalism is, then, the truth that rational beings externalize their costs when they lack the motive to act otherwise. The conservative response is to find the needed motive. When people in Britain began to become conscious of the environment, and of the reckless way that they were destroying it, the principal object of their concern was the forest – the Greenwood of the Robin Hood myth, celebrated in much of the popular poetry and song of Shakespeare's day, and made into a *cause célèbre* by John Evelyn in his book *Silva, or a Discourse on Forestation*, first published in 1664. It was another 200 years before the environmental movement began in earnest, though English art, literature and religion had by then made the saving of the landscape into one of its perennial themes. When the movement really took off it was in reaction to the Industrial Revolution, and its leading light, John Ruskin, described himself as a Tory, rather than a Liberal or a socialist – although such labels are always misleading when applied to genuinely intelligent people.

Environmental protection entered English law in 1865, with the leading case in tort of *Rylands* v. *Fletcher*. This established a regime of strict liability, so that the one whose activity causes the damage is the one who must compensate the victims. This was a judgement of the courts under common-law principles, and not the work of Parliament. The same happened a century later when the Anglers Association used common-law principles to obtain judgement against the major river polluters, who were local governments and nationalized power suppliers.[3] In general we should be aware of, and protective towards, those precious legal instruments that we already possess, and which often depend on principles of equity and natural law and not on top-down legislation.

But has not environmentalism awoken us also to another truth, concerning the interconnectedness of all that happens in our environment, and the impossibility of rectifying externalities merely by looking at our own particular patch? No event in the universe is insulated from the causal network in which everything is bound: and the eco-systems of our globe are respecters neither of national boundaries nor of historical attachments. In response to that observation, environmental activists tend to look for treaties, international committees and transnational regulators – in short, bureaucracies with no

---

[3] I discuss these cases and the reasoning behind them in *Green Philosophy: How to Think Seriously about the Planet* (London: Atlantic Books, and New York: Oxford University Press, 2012), Chapter 5.

attachment to the places over which they exert their power, but with an internationally acknowledged remit.

That response is understandable, but it suffers from crucial defects, and these defects are increasingly evident in the situation that confronts us now. It is true that the nations of the world willingly signed up to the Montreal Protocol on Ozone Depleting Substances. In that case, the benefits were immediate, and not delayed for decades (as would be the case for any agreement over greenhouse gas emissions). The technology to replace the harmful emissions was already being developed in the private sector, and in accepting the agreement no nation incurred large costs or risked disrupting the life of its citizens. Such a treaty certainly casts a ray of hope through the fog of our uncertainties. But it should be seen as an exception rather than the rule. When it comes to the real megaproblems, we should recognize that the disposition to obey treaties when they are not in the signatory's interest is a rare feature of political systems. It comes about only in states built from a tradition of accountability – in other words the nation states, in which the sovereignty of the people is acknowledged by the institutions of government. Among the big polluters it is certain that the United States would obey a treaty when the cost of doing so is felt; uncertain that India would do so; certain that China would defect.

In the light of this, it seems to me, we should recognize that the problem of climate change that occupies international negotiations today is not in fact a diplomatic problem. It is primarily a scientific problem: the problem of discovering a cheap and effective source of clean energy that will remove both the cost of signing up to a treaty and the motive to defect from it. The solution to this scientific problem is indeed more likely to be found through international cooperation – but cooperation among scientists, not among states.

True, scientists need funding. Research is often funded by private enterprises, which hope to use the result in order to gain a competitive edge. But no existing business has, in that way, an interest in clean energy sufficient to fund the massive research needed to discover it. Hence it is through government funding that this research must proceed, and that means funding from governments sufficiently wealthy and sufficiently public spirited to commit the necessary resources. There is only one nation in the world that has the economic strength, the adaptability, the accountability to its citizens, and the political will to address the problem of clean energy. And that nation – the United States of America – is passing through an extended economic crisis at the very moment when the greatest need is for the costly research and far-reaching policies that only the United States can afford and that, indeed, only the United States has the political will to pursue. So far, none of the nation states most responsible for greenhouse gas emissions have been able to meet reduction targets – whether self-imposed or accepted under the Kyoto Protocol. The reason for this is clear: any far-reaching policy requires energy for its implementation. And if the only energy available is carbon-based, no policy aimed at a substantial reduction in carbon emissions can succeed. Only the discovery of affordable clean energy can solve the problem, and until that discovery is made, all treaties will be interim measures at best.

Such treaties may nevertheless be necessary. But they have to be realistic, and founded on the known proclivities of the signatories. The reluctance of the left to acknowledge the truth about communism infects also its attitude to modern China, where the destruction of the environment proceeds at a frightening pace, and where economic, social and political systems have been wrenched free of their old forms of homeostasis, and set on a one-way path to catastrophe. Meanwhile we should acknowledge that the search for climate-change treaties, conducted as it is in an atmosphere of scientific uncertainty, interrupted by moments of blind panic, uses up the sparse treaty-making power of nations on a problem that no treaty can presently solve. It therefore leads us to ignore the problems that *could* be solved – such as the overfishing of breeding grounds, the destruction of biodiversity by pesticides and the mad use of packaging, which is leading to the death from plastic of the oceans.

It could not possibly be part of a conservative response to global warming simply to say: let nothing change. On the contrary, a great many things *must* change if we are to live with the unprecedented prosperity, longevity and repro-ductive success that make our species such a burden to the planet. However, we are being invited to extract climate change from the pile of our environmental problems and to exalt it above all the others. The effect is to neutralize our rooted and temperate ways of accommodating change. The assumption is that we are dealing with a new kind and a new order of change, and one to which we *cannot* adapt. And if that is so it would of course mark a serious departure for our species, which has survived by adapting, and which has added to the list of its biological adaptations an enormous coda of social and political adaptations, of which the market economy, the rule of law, scientific method and religion are but four, responsible between them for the vast expansion of our species and therefore for our current environmental problems. It is the thought that all our adaptations – biological, social, cultural and spiritual – may now be ineffective that is so disturbing. But this thought is in no way supported by the recent history of environmental change. 'Resilience solutions', therefore, ought to be part of the repertoire of every thinking environmentalist.

Consider the transformations that occurred in Britain during the nineteenth century, when our populations moved en masse to the manufacturing cities and whole areas of the countryside were abandoned. Early observers like William Cobbett prophesied a complete collapse of agriculture and a spoiling of the landscape, together with a losing battle against moral corruption, disease and enslavement in the growing conurbations. Within two generations, however, people were beginning to adapt to this new environment. New and less labour-intensive forms of agriculture emerged, while reforms in the law of settled land made it possible for entrepreneurial farmers to buy self-sufficient sections of the moribund estates. The harnessing of energy from coal eventually brought an unprecedented rise in the standard of living not only in the towns but across the country, as the railways began to link the towns and to bring employment and markets to the places between them.

Although political decisions helped the process of adaptation, they did not initiate it, and were themselves the result of campaigns and movements that originated in civil society. British society adapted to the Industrial Revolution in the same way as it had set the Revolution in motion: by private enterprise and civil association. Already by the end of the eighteenth century the Friendly Societies – charitable foundations offering mortgages to low-income families – had begun to address the problem of crowding and homelessness in the cities. During the next 50 years, the network of Anglican and Nonconformist schools expanded to offer education to a majority of the nation's children. Thanks to charitable initiatives, including the foundation in 1832 of the British Medical Association, the health of the population rapidly improved. Philanthropic agitation led to the Factory Acts, the first of which was passed in 1802. These (notably the Act of 1844) countered the worst abuses and compelled employers of children both to limit their hours of work and to ensure that they acquired a basic education. By the end of the century, new centres of civilization, like Victorian Manchester and Leeds, had become home to all their residents, to be celebrated in our art and literature and fully integrated into the affections of the people.

The process that led to the growth of those cities was prodigal of hardships, injustices and ill health, and received biting commentary from Dickens in the description of Coketown (*Hard Times*, 1869). But it was equally rich in faith, hope and charity, and in the environmental initiatives that led, among other things, to the public control of sanitation and waste. Some of these initiatives resulted in legislation; some came about through the common law of tort. The whole process provides an exemplary illustration of the way in which civil society, acting in conjunction with an accountable legislature, adjusts to environmental change, and manages change in the interests of its members. Commentators like Mrs Gaskell and Charles Dickens had no equivalent in previous centuries, not because things were better then, but because they were worse. The factories liberated children from the farms, where they were worked just as hard and with less hope of rescue. Children working in factories came under the eye of educated people who could afford the luxury of compassion, and within a few decades the Factory Acts had rescued them from slavery.

Surely we should not rule out the hope of adapting to climate change in a way similar to that exemplified by the response to the Industrial Revolution? Of course, if the prophecies of the alarmists are fulfilled, adaptation will not be possible. Old England will survive only in the way it survives in the taxi-driver's diary that is the subtext of Will Self's novel *The Book of Dave*. Many European and American cities grew as London and Bristol did, as outlets to the sea and to the goods that trade by sea. If sea levels rise, such cities will be affected in ways that will be both costly and painful. But what would enable us to adapt to the change? Surely the very thing that enabled us to adapt to the Industrial Revolution, namely the growth of new forms of local attachment, new forms of civil association, new ways of cooperating with our neighbours in free and law-abiding groups. Either the changes that are to come will be manageable or they will not. And if they are manageable it is because our inherent social motives can embrace them, and not because the state has some power that we don't have, to manage them on our behalf.

So what is the answer? Not vindictiveness but trusteeship; not unenforceable treaties but real examples of successful stewardship; not the attack on markets, but the use of markets to restore equilibrium. The truth in environmentalism therefore points to the reasonableness of conservatism, and to the need to incorporate the aim of stewardship into conservative policies.

As with the other truths I have been discussing, however, the truth in environmentalism can be leaned on until it becomes a falsehood, and as with the other instances this transition from truth to falsehood occurs when the religious impulse displaces the political. The environmental issue has been presented, by activist NGOs and by Green politicians, as a confrontation between the force of

darkness and the force of light. The force of darkness corresponds to the traditional target of left-wing criticism: big business, the market and the 'greed' and
'selfishness' that are destroying us. Against those powerful forces are aligned
the forces of light: activists, NGOs, people animated by a selfless concern for
future generations rather than the pursuit of their own comfort. And, because
such people do not enjoy the enormous institutional and economic power of
their opponents, they must call on another and higher force to represent them,
the force of the state, which can use the law to overbear the selfish behaviour of
those who would otherwise destroy the planet.

Once it is presented in that way, with all the ideological embellishments with
which we are familiar, the left-wing position calls into being by its very logic a
right-wing position, which defends individual freedom and markets against the
bogeyman of state control and top-down dictatorship. And as the ideological
conflict heats up, all kinds of thing are put in question that ought not to be put
in question, facts are fabricated and research politicized, and the legitimate use
of the state and the legitimate sphere of private enterprise are both lost sight
of in the flurry of accusations. The lesson that conservatives should take from
this is the same as the lesson they should take from the other mass movements
of solidarity that I have mentioned. They should learn from the conflicts over
the environment that political solutions emerge from below and are shaped
by the motives of real people. They are not imposed from above by those who
regard their fellow humans with suspicion, and who long to replace them with
something better.

9

The Truth in Internationalism

Conservatism is not, by nature, internationalist, and is suspicious of all attempts to control the legislation and government of the country from a place beyond its borders. It acknowledges the truth in liberalism, that the political process can be founded in consent only if it acknowledges the rights of the individual. But opposition, disagreement, the free expression of provocative views and the rule of compromise all presuppose a shared identity.

I have argued that the kind of first-person plural that we need, in order to protect the rights of opposition and the politics of compromise, is a national rather than a religious 'we'. Unless and until people identify themselves with the country, its territory and its cultural inheritance – in something like the way people identify themselves with a family – the politics of compromise will not emerge. As I argued in Chapter 3, people have to take their neighbours seriously, as people with an equal claim to protection, for whom they might be required, in moments of crisis, to face mortal danger.

Inevitably, therefore, conservatives will look askance at attempts to legislate from a place outside the jurisdiction, and will need persuading before signing a treaty that renounces or diminishes sovereignty in some matter of vital national concern. The many projects for global governance, or for radically diminishing the sovereignty of nation states, are apt to be rejected by conservatives as utopian, since they propose a new kind of citizenship based in no pre-political tie. They are seeking for a political order without the attachment that would make it possible. So, at least, does it seem.

But we must acknowledge the truth in internationalism. The resolution of disputes between sovereigns by treaty rather than by force is of ancient provenance, and during the late Middle Ages attempts were made to extract a kind of common law of nations from the assumptions that underlie treaty-making. Grotius's great work, *De Jure belli ac pacis* (1625) – on the law of war and peace – was an attempt to adapt principles of natural law to the government of affairs between sovereign states. Grotius laid the foundations for international law as we now know it. Kant, in his short discourse on *Perpetual Peace*, acknowledged that international law would always be defective if there were no way of enforcing it short of war. He therefore advocated a 'League of Nations', in which the various nation states draw up an agreement to hand over their disputes to a central body, in which all are represented, but which has the power to adjudicate disputes between them. This suggestion led to the foundation of the short-lived League of Nations following the First World War, and the United Nations Organization after the Second World War. And although there are many things to be criticized in the UN, and although its institutions and procedures are not, in the nature of the case, proof against capture by rogue states and tyrants masquerading as legitimate sovereigns, it is widely agreed that the existence of this organization has contributed to the resolution of many conflicts that might otherwise have got out of hand.

The truth in internationalism is that sovereign states are legal persons, and should deal with each other through a system of rights, duties, liabilities and responsibilities: in other words, through the 'calculus of rights and duties' to which I referred in Chapter 6. They should enter into voluntary agreements that have the force of contracts in law, and these agreements should be binding on successive governments in just the way that contracts entered into by a firm bind its successive directors. To make these dealings possible, states must be sovereign – that is, able to decide matters for themselves – and also willing to relinquish powers to those bodies charged with maintaining international agreements and the law that governs them.

So much is common sense. But it is not what internationalism now amounts to. Once again a fundamental truth has been captured by people with an agenda, and so turned to falsehood. This transformation of the internationalist idea has influenced not only the UN but, more concretely, the EU and the European Court of Human Rights, both institutions that arose from the European wars, as a result of pressure from utopian internationalists.

The idea of European integration, in its current form, was conceived during the First World War, became a political reality in the wake of the Second, and is marked by the conflicts that gave birth to it. It seemed reasonable, even imperative, in 1950 to bring the nations of Europe together, in a way that would prevent the wars that had twice almost destroyed the continent. And because conflicts breed radicalism, the new Europe was conceived as a comprehensive plan – one that would eliminate the sources of European conflict, and place cooperation rather than rivalry at the heart of the continental order.

The architects of the plan, who were for the most part Christian Democrats, had little else in common apart from a belief in European civilization and a distrust of the nation state. The *eminence grise,* Jean Monnet, was a transnational bureaucrat, inspired by the vision of a united Europe in which war would be a thing of the past. His close collaborator, Walter Hallstein, was an academic German technocrat, who believed in international jurisdiction as the natural successor to the laws of the nation states. Monnet and Hallstein were joined by Altiero Spinelli, a romantic communist who advocated a United States of Europe legitimized by a democratically elected European parliament. Such people were not isolated enthusiasts, but part of a broad movement among the post-war political class. They chose popular leaders like Konrad Adenauer, Robert Schuman and Alcide De Gasperi as the spokesmen for their ideas, and proposed the European Coal and Steel Community (the Schuman Plan) as their initial goal – believing that the larger project would acquire legitimacy if it could first be understood and accepted in this circumscribed form.

I do not wish to deny the achievements of those public-spirited people. However, we should remember that when the first instruments of European cooperation were being devised, our continent was divided by the Iron Curtain, with half of Germany and all of the Slavic countries under Soviet occupation and fascist regimes installed in Portugal and Spain. France was in constant turmoil, with a Communist Party commanding the support of more than a third of its electorate; the free remnant of Europe was critically dependent upon the Atlantic alliance, and the marks of occupation and defeat were (except in Great Britain and the Iberian peninsula) everywhere apparent. Only radical measures, it seemed, could restore the continent to political and economic health, and those measures must replace the old antagonisms with a new spirit of friendship. As a result, European integration was conceived in one-dimensional terms, as a process of ever-increasing *unity*, under a centralized structure of command. Each increase in central power was to be matched by a diminution of national power. Every summit, every directive and every ratcheted click of the *acquis communautaire* has since carried within itself this specific equation. And because we have reached a new turning point for Europe, we must now consider the results.

We have undeniably gained much since those days: material prosperity, longevity, health and security from external threat. And those benefits have been furthered by the international institutions established in the wake of the Second World War – for example by the UN peacekeeping efforts, by NATO, to the existence of which we owe the collapse of the Soviet Union, and by the General Agreements on Tariffs and Trade (GATT – now superseded by the WTO). The European institutions have had an equal part to play. By providing stable links to the surrounding world, they have facilitated the democratization of countries previously subject to fascist or communist dictatorship; and by binding France and Germany together they have stabilized those two countries, both internally and externally.

However, we should also recognize that conditions have changed, and that instruments for dealing with the problems of 50 years ago are not necessarily suited to the problems of today. Although the Soviet empire has collapsed, it has left a legacy of political distrust and covert lawlessness that can be overcome only by a strengthening, rather than a weakening, of national attachments. Europe's rapidly diminishing share of the world's trade and wealth bespeaks a shift in power of a kind that is only seen every few centuries. Mass immigrations from Africa, Asia and the Middle East have created potentially disloyal, and in any case anti-national, minorities in the heart of France, Germany, the Netherlands, the Scandinavian countries and Britain. The Christian faith has receded from public life, leaving a vacuum into which nihilism, materialism and militant Islam have flowed unresisted. The population is getting older and sparser – except in Britain, which is the destination of choice for so many European migrants, and now in deep conflict as a result. In confronting those ills, which define the new crisis of Europe as surely as the rise of totalitarianism defined the old one, the exclusive emphasis on 'integration' is at best an irrelevance, at worst a fatal mistake.

However radical our vision of Europe's future, we shall have to depend on the nation states for its realization. By replacing national accountability with distant bureaucracy, the machinery of the EU has left us disarmed and bewildered in the face of our current crisis. Its constant seizure of powers and privileges without any reciprocal attempt to account for their exercise is undermining all trust in the political process. By constantly going against the deeply rooted diversity of the European nations, the project of 'ever closer union' has not merely alienated the people of Europe, but has shown its inability to tap the true resources and the creative potential of our people, and to revitalize the idea of European civilization.

It is true that Bismarck brought the German principalities together by imposing a unified system of law and a centrally administered bureaucracy. And in all probability Bismarck's success has inspired those like Jacques Delors, who have wished to achieve a similar unification across Europe. But Bismarck's intention was to create a nation state; he began from the assumption of shared language, shared customs and historically vindicated borders. In his *Kulturkampf* against the Catholic Church he made it clear that he wished to neutralize transnational sources of authority, and not to endorse them. To think that this project of 'unity through regulation' can succeed outside Bismarck's professed goal of nation-building is surely naïve. Bismarck was not merely creating a unified political structure; he was creating a new centre of loyalty, one that subsumed the traditional allegiances of the German-speaking peoples, and gave them a shared identity in the emerging industrial world. The European Union has made half-hearted attempts to appropriate to itself the loyalties and identities of the European nations; but the futility of the task, and the absurdity of its expression, have merely reminded the people of Europe that laws made in Brussels are laws made by *others*, who are outside the allegiance that binds the nation together.

The integrationists have attempted to soothe the growing discontent among the people with the doctrine of 'subsidiarity'. This word, incorporated into the Maastricht Treaty, and ostensibly guaranteeing local sovereignty, was given its current sense in an encyclical of Pope Pius XI in 1931, describing the decentralization of power as a fundamental item of the social doctrine of the Church. According to Pius XI, 'subsidiarity' means that decisions are taken always at the lowest level compatible with the overarching authority of government. The term was appropriated by Wilhelm Röpke, the German economist who, exiled from Nazi Germany in Switzerland, was amazed and encouraged to discover a society which is the opposite in so many ways to the one from which he had escaped.[1] He saw that Swiss society is organized from the bottom up, and resolves its problems at the local level, through the free association of citizens in those 'little platoons' to which Edmund Burke had made such a passionate appeal when decrying the top-down dictatorship of the French Revolution. Subsidiarity, in Röpke's understanding of the term, refers to the right of local communities to take decisions for themselves, including the decision to surrender the matter to a higher forum. Subsidiarity places an absolute brake upon centralizing powers, by permitting their involvement only when requested. It is the way to reconcile a market economy with the local loyalties and public spirit that it might otherwise erode.

---

[1]   Wilhelm Röpke, *A Humane Economy: The Social Framework of the Free Market* (London: O. Wolff, 1960).

In the EU as it is today, the term 'subsidiarity' denotes not the means whereby powers are passed up from the bottom, but the means whereby powers are allocated from the top. It is the EU and its institutions that decides where subsidiary powers begin and end, and by purporting to grant powers in the very word that removes them, the term 'subsidiarity' wraps the whole idea of decentralized government in mystery. For the Eurocrats, national governments are autonomous only at the 'subsidiary' level, with the European institutions uniquely empowered to determine which level that is. It is hardly surprising if the Swiss people, observing the effect of this, have, in defiance of their political class, persistently refused to join the European Union.

Conservatives are advocates of subsidiarity, meaning by the term what Röpke meant, and also what Publius (Alexander Hamilton) meant, in defending the 'federal' constitution of the United States, namely: a political arrangement in which 'power is granted by liberty, and not liberty by power'.[2] How to achieve this arrangement, so as to restore accountability, flexibility and competitive advantage to the European Union, is a question that cannot be easily solved. However, without a genuine form of subsidiarity, I believe, there can be no real future for the European Union, which will fragment under the pressure of its top-heavy legislative burden and the disruptive effects of mass migration – effects which have already led to a powerful movement for secession in Britain.

The crisis to which the institutions of Europe were a first response was the result of one thing above all – the centralized and dictatorial approach to politics, exemplified in the Nazi Party's warmongering, in the Communist Party's totalitarian control, and in the fascist grip on Italy and Spain. The EU has benign origins and noble intentions that can bear no comparison with those vanished agendas. Yet it is this same dictatorial approach that has been built into the European process, which has one and only one way forward, namely 'more laws, more rules, more government, more power to the centre'. The dangers attendant on this concentration of powers are not aggressive, military or totalitarian. They are subtle and insidious: the dangers of civic alienation, of a loss of economic competitiveness, and of the domination of decision-making by an increasingly unaccountable elite.

---

[2] 'Publius' was the pseudonym adopted by Alexander Hamilton, James Madison and John Jay in *The Federalist*, first published in two volumes in 1788. The quotation is from Hamilton, in Letter 39.

National sovereignty is a precondition of democracy. And national sovereignty involves the right to determine who resides within the national borders, who controls the nation's assets, and who is entitled to the advantages of citizenship. It presupposes a 'we' from which our bargaining begins and whose interests that bargaining serves. Treaties between sovereign states need not involve a loss of autonomy, any more than a contract between individuals involves a loss of freedom. On the contrary, contract and treaty are both expressions of sovereignty, and the axiom that *pacta sunt servanda* (agreements are to be honoured) is, like Kant's categorical imperative, a law expressing the freedom of those who are bound by it.

The Treaty of Rome could, if interpreted in the spirit in which it was originally signed, still function as a willed expression of the sovereignty of its signatories. For if individual autonomy is a precondition of the free market, so is national sovereignty a precondition of free trade. As now interpreted, however, the Treaty goes beyond any conventional interpretation of how treaties operate, and has become an irreversible surrender, more akin to a marriage than a contract. When regulation can penetrate to the very heart of economic competitors, extinguishing the customs that make each the individual that it is, then what you have is not free trade between sovereign nations, but the abolition of nations, and therefore of the trade between them. This is perhaps what Jean Monnet intended; but it is not how the European project was sold to the people. Globalization has not diminished people's sense of nationhood: under its impact, the nations have become the chosen and prime receptacles of citizens' trust, and the indispensable means to understand and enjoy the new condition of our world.

By means of the EU legislative machine, a country whose economy has been crippled by laws regarding the hours and conditions of work can export the cost of those laws by imposing them on its competitors. Or a country can lobby for regulations that favour native financial institutions over their foreign rivals. These things are happening continually in the EU process, to the extent that it is no longer at all clear whether trade between the nation states of Europe has been furthered or hampered by the regulative regime. All that is certain is that the economic life of Europe is increasingly controlled from the centre. And this process damages the real interests of all the European peoples, by making Europe as a whole less and less competitive with the wider world.

So how should trade between the European nation states be organized, and what kind of legislative regime will reconcile national sovereignty with the free flow of goods and services, while promoting the good neighbourly relations that Europe needs? We cannot, by regulation alone, reconcile the diverse interests and identities of our continent, nor should we try to do so. When nations agree to lower the barriers to reciprocal trade, they surrender only those powers that would-be trading partners object to – powers to alter tariffs or non-tariff barriers, for example, or to intervene in mergers and competition. If the partners insist on retaining their own laws regarding working hours, pensions, employment rights, religious holidays or whatever, then this is their right as sovereign entities. Negotiations without safeguards for assets that have been ring-fenced as fundamental to *who we are*, involve an abrogation of the very thing that makes free negotiation possible, namely the autonomy of the partners. This elementary truth, which is no more than a truth of logic, is perfectly compatible with the existence of Europe-wide treaties of free trade, and a European court of justice empowered to adjudicate disputes under those treaties. But it is not compatible with the kind of legislative machine established by the European Commission, with the enforced dissolution of national borders or with the emergence of unaccountable government occupied by an elite of political has-beens.

The question in everybody's mind is how such a huge mistake can be rectified? The worst mistake in politics is the mistake made by Lenin – the mistake of destroying the institutions and procedures whereby mistakes can be recognized. Something similar is happening to the EU, whose elites, faced with the growing problems posed by popular discontent, mass migration, the troubled single currency and the collapse of the peripheral economies, respond with the single cry: more Europe. In other words: not backwards to what we know, but forwards into the void. The astonishing thing is that our elected representatives have left it to the eleventh hour to say what they should have said 30 years ago, which is not more Europe, but less.

Suppose the nations of Europe are able to recapture their sovereignty, however. What should be their relationship, and the relationship of free democracies generally, to the rest of the world? Two rival views of international relations now compete for influence among our political elites, the 'national' and the 'transnational', and recent events in the Middle East have sharpened the conflict between them. According to the national view, the business of politics is to maintain law, order, peace, freedom and security within the borders of a sovereign state. The way to maintain peace, in the national view, is to uphold national sovereignty in every area where it might be threatened, and to maintain a balance of power among neighbours. Threatening behaviour from any foreign state must be met with a counter-threat sufficient to deter aggression. And wherever possible, the balance of power must be supplemented by pacts of non-aggression and treaties recognizing common interests – provided only that such treaties do not weaken or compromise national sovereignty. The First World War, with its senseless slaughter and incomprehensible goals, discredited, in the minds of many people, that 'balance of power' approach to conflict. The League of Nations was founded with the express purpose of replacing the national view with a transnational alternative.

According to the transnational view, belligerence between sovereign states cannot be prevented by the threat of force but only by a rule of law. Disputes between states should be resolved in the same way as disputes between citizens – namely, by recourse to law and the imposition of a judgement. This will require transnational government, with law-making and law-enforcing institutions. The authority habitually cited in defence of this approach is Kant.[3] Under Kant's proposed League of Nations, sovereign nations would submit to a common jurisdiction, to be enforced by sanctions.

What Kant had in mind, however, was very far from transnational government as it is now conceived. He was adamant that there can be no guarantee of peace unless the powers acceding to the treaty are republics. Republican government, as defined by Kant, both here and elsewhere in his political writings, means representative government under a rule of law,[4] and his League is one that binds self-governing and sovereign nations, whose peoples enjoy the rights and duties of citizenship. For Kant, the kind of international law that is needed for peace 'presupposes the separate existence of many independent states … [united under] a federal union to prevent hostilities breaking out'. This state of affairs is to be preferred to 'an amalgamation of the separate nations under a single power'.[5] And he then gives the principal objection to transnational government, namely that 'laws progressively lose their impact as the government increases its range, and a soulless despotism, after crushing the germs of goodness, will finally lapse into anarchy'.[6]

[3] Immanuel Kant, *Perpetual Peace*, in Hans Reiss, ed., *Kant: Political Writings*, 2nd edn. (Cambridge: Cambridge University Press, 1991).

[4] Ibid., p. 99f., where Kant gives one of several definitions, none of which exactly coincides with any other, but all of which point in the same direction.

[5] Ibid., p. 113.

[6] Ibid.

It seems then that Kant can be taken only as partly endorsing transnational government as we now know it. His League of Nations could be a reality, he thought, only if the states united by it were genuinely sovereign, genuinely representative of their people and genuinely governed by law. This is manifestly not the case of a great many members of the UN today, and certainly not the case of those, like North Korea, which have posed the greatest threat to their immediate neighbours. Such states are not really sovereign bodies, but rather conscript armies in the hands of thugs.[7] Power is exercised by those thugs not by representative government, still less by law, but by the machinery of one-party dictatorship, supplemented by mafia clientism and family ties. Advocates of Kantian internationalism are therefore caught in a dilemma. If law is to be effective in the resolution of conflicts, all parties must be law-abiding members of the community of nations. What are we to do, then, with the rogue state? Are we entitled to depose its rulers, so as to change subjects to citizens, rulers to representatives and force to law? If not, are we to regard ourselves as *really* bound by laws and treaties by which the rogue state merely *pretends* to be bound? In which case, what guarantee do those laws and treaties offer of a 'perpetual peace'?

Kant's caveats notwithstanding, advocates of the transnational idea have persistently maintained that all disputes between states ought to be submitted to international law, and that belligerence can never be justified until all legal channels have been thoroughly explored and exhausted. This position has been maintained even when one party to the dispute is an entirely despotic or totalitarian power, which rules by force but not by law. For, it is maintained, such a power can be compelled to abide by its obligations under international law by sanctions, and sanctions fall short of belligerence, since they respect the sovereignty and independence of the state against which they are enforced.

Now there is no doubt that sanctions hurt the people of the states to which they are applied. Shortages of vital supplies, collapse of export- and import-dependent businesses, the general undermining of social relations by the black market, all serve to spread poverty and distrust among the people, leading to hardship and even – so it was claimed of Saddam's Iraq – starvation. But, for that very reason, sanctions are as likely to enhance as to deplete the power of the ruling elite. The Kim family and its clients have benefited enormously

---

[7]   In the case of North Korea, Christopher Hitchens has plausibly argued, not a conscript army but a concentration camp, in the hands of a family of madmen. See Christopher Hitchens, *Arguably* (London: Atlantic Books, 2011), pp. 553–8.

from the starvation that they have inflicted on the North Korean people, and the cooperation of the international community in ensuring that the North Koreans live without hope has been only one more gift to the ruling tyranny. The privations endured by the North Koreans mean that they have neither the strength nor the mutual trust to challenge their oppressors. The same was true of Saddam's Iraq. Moreover, Saddam's circle of Ba'athist thugs enriched itself through smuggling and the black market, just as the party elite in Soviet Russia enriched itself through the deprivations of the Soviet people. Sanctions make a substantial contribution to power based on privation, and can undermine a tyranny only when it is dependent in some way on the well-being of its subjects.

Furthermore, the inherent corruption of transnational bureaucracies ensures that the UN has become a channel for escaping law rather than a means to impose it. Saddam, it seems, was able to use the massive flow of money under the ancillary 'oil for food' programme to enrich not only himself and his cronies but also his foreign supporters, without in any way improving the lot of the poor Iraqis who were the intended beneficiaries of the deal. Indeed it proved easier for the Iraqi elite to fatten themselves through oil sales constrained by sanctions than through peacetime sales on the open market.[8]

Those are not the only negative effects of sanctions, however. By helping to maintain the fiction of a 'legal' route to the goal of compliance, sanctions postpone the force that might be required to reach it. Of course, international law recognizes the legitimate use of force – in particular to counter aggression or repel invasion. But it always sets strict limits to its use, seeing force as a last resort whose purpose is to rectify force used by others. Hence the United States obtained the endorsement of the UN for the first Gulf War on the understanding that the intention was to expel the invader from Kuwait. But any further action, such as the invasion of Iraq and the deposing of Saddam Hussein, remained illegal. The United States respected the law, so creating the conditions in which Saddam could reassert his grip over the Iraqi people, and punish those, like the residents of Basra, who had been briefly misled into thinking that the tyrant's time was up. Once again, international law acted to postpone the resolution of a conflict, and by preventing the march on Baghdad, ensured that the march would occur only in circumstances far less likely to minimize the loss of life or to gain the consent of the Iraqi people.

Kant's *Perpetual Peace* proposed an international jurisdiction with one

---

8   Report by Claude Hankes-Drielsma to Congress, 21 April 2004.

purpose only – to secure peace between neighbouring jurisdictions. The League of Nations broke down because the background presupposition was not fulfilled – namely, that its members should be republics, bound together by citizenship and the rule of law. (The rise of totalitarian government in Russia and Germany meant the abolition of citizenship in those countries; and it was those countries that were the aggressors in the Second World War.) The defenders of transnational government have cheerfully ignored Kant's presupposition. Worse, they have also ignored Kant's restriction of international jurisdiction to the goal of peace. Our national jurisdictions are now bombarded by laws from outside, even though hardly any of these laws are concerned with the avoidance of war. We, the citizens, are powerless in the matter, and they, the legislators, entirely unanswerable to us, who must obey them. This is exactly what Kant dreaded, as the sure path, first to despotism and then to anarchy. The growth of the transnational view of conflict-resolution has therefore led to a serious tying of the hands – not of the lawless states whose hands may need tying but can never be tied by law, but of the law-abiding democracies. We, who regard ourselves as bound by our treaties, are also bound to lose their benefits.

One instance of this deserves mention, since it is a major contribution to the loss of security in Europe. The Geneva Convention on Refugees and Asylum was ratified in 1951, when there were no refugees uncatered for in Europe and very few applicants for asylum – a fact which meant that there was no cost involved in ratifying the convention. This has bound the legislatures of the nation states ever since, despite radically changed circumstances. The convention enables dictators to export their opponents without earning the bad name that comes from killing them. The entire cost of the convention is therefore borne by the law-abiding states. An uneasy silence has so far prevailed concerning this, one of the most important issues facing modern Europe. Many of those claiming asylum bring with them the Islamist frenzies of the countries from which they have escaped. Some claim the benefits of citizenship, even sue for them as 'human rights', while acknowledging no duty to the state in return. There are now British citizens engaged in a jihad against the British people[9] for whom

---

[9]   The case of *al-muhajiroun* is now sufficiently notorious – see John Marks and Caroline Cox, *The 'West', Islam and Islamism* (London: Civitas, 2003) and my *The West and the Rest* (Wilmington, DE: ISI Books, 2002). It is only one case of many, however, all of which illustrate what happens to citizenship when it is detached from the national idea. Citizenship is bought and sold like a forged passport, to become a tax on other people's loyalty.

the accusation of treason is as incomprehensible as the suggestion that there is treason on the moon. Should we not deal with this problem by consulting the national interest, rather than surrendering to a treaty signed before most of us were born?

Internationalists tend to be cosmopolitans, who identify themselves as 'world citizens', and consciously repudiate the old national loyalties that bind them to a particular nation, a particular country and a particular jurisdiction. However, it could be that the national perspective is more favourable to national security and also to world order than a philosophy that construes all people everywhere on the model of the armchair liberal. Nationalism, construed as a belligerent assertion of the nation's 'rights' against its neighbours, has certainly been a destructive force in European politics, as I indicated in Chapter 3. But nation states, in which constitutional and democratic procedures rest on national attachment, have, on the whole, been peaceful members of the international community. Although the border between Canada and the United States is disputed, and has been disputed for a century or more, the chances that this dispute will lead to war are zero. The national perspective encourages realistic assumptions about the sympathies, budgets, energies and intellects of human beings. It assumes that the people for which it speaks are citizens, whose consent must be won to any act of belligerence, and who vastly prefer negotiation and compromise to intransigence and war.

If the democracies are to protect themselves against the growing threats to them, therefore, it is as necessary as it ever was to take the national rather than the transnational perspective. Globalization, easy travel and the removal of barriers to migration have changed the nature of the threat. But they have not changed the effective response to it, which is, as Clausewitz taught us, to disarm the enemy so that we can impose our will. The enemy is now hidden in global networks. But this makes the international approach not more useful to us, but less. Enemies can be confronted only if they are first brought to earth. And that means bringing them to earth *somewhere*, as the Americans brought al-Qaʻeda to earth in Afghanistan. Globalization may have made it harder to defend ourselves against terrorist assaults, but we are nevertheless defending territory, the place where we are, and hunting down our enemies in the place where *they* are.

That observation reminds us of another, and to me decisive, point in favour of a national approach to conflict. The cosmopolitan outlook of Marxism-Leninism justified the Soviet occupation of Eastern Europe for 40 years. The anti-national vision of the Islamists encourages aspiring *mujahidoun* to join those who are trying to impose Islamic government around the world, regardless of whether the local people consent to it. By contrast, powers that enter war in order to defend national territory need have only one intention, which is to withdraw from the conflict when the battle is won – as the Americans and their allies are currently trying to withdraw from Afghanistan. Such powers are in a position to recognize that the age of empire is over, and that conflict will cease only when nations, obedient to the will of their people, agree the terms on which they can coexist. That is the direction in which conservatives wish the world to go; and one major obstacle is the internationalist desire to dissolve all borders and to govern the world from nowhere.

10

The Truth in Conservatism

Conservatism is not in the business of correcting human nature or shaping it according to some conception of the ideal rational chooser. It attempts to understand how societies work, and to make the space required for them to work successfully. Its starting point is the deep psychology of the human person. Its fundamental philosophy has never been better captured than by Hegel in the *Phenomenology of Spirit*, which shows how self-consciousness and freedom emerge through the venture out from the self towards the other; how relations of conflict and domination are overcome by the recognition of mutual rights and duties, and how, in the course of this, the individual achieves not only freedom of action but also a sense of his own and others' value. The process whereby human beings acquire their freedom also builds their attachments, and the institutions of law, education and politics are part of this – not things that we freely choose from a position of detachment, but things through which we *acquire* our freedom, and without which we could not exist as fully self-conscious agents.

I leave it to the interested reader to decipher Hegel's argument in detail.[1] What emerges from it is the view of human beings as accountable to each other, bound in associations of mutual responsibility and finding fulfilment in the family and the life of civil society. Our existence as citizens, freely participating in the *polis*, is made possible by our enduring attachments to the things we hold dear. Our condition is not that of *Homo oeconomicus*, searching in everything to satisfy his private desires. We are home-building creatures, cooperating in the search for intrinsic values, and what matters to us are the ends, not the means, of our existence.

---

[1] I offer a little help, however, in 'Hegel as a Conservative Thinker', in *Philosopher on Dover Beach* (South Bend, IN: St Augustine's Press, 1998).

Association and Discrimination

The truth in conservatism lies in those thoughts. Free association is necessary to us, not only because 'no man is an island', but because intrinsic values emerge from social cooperation. They are not imposed by some outside authority or instilled through fear. They grow from below, through relations of love, respect and accountability. The fallacy of thinking that we can plan for a society in which fulfilment is readily available, dispensed to all-comers by a benign bureaucracy, is not one that I need here attack.[2] The important point is that what matters to us comes through our own efforts at constructing it, and seldom if ever from above, except in those emergencies in which a top-down command is indispensable.

From the raw material of human affection, we construct enduring associations, with their rules, offices, ceremonies and hierarchies that endow our activities with intrinsic worth. Schools, churches, libraries; choirs, orchestras, bands, theatre groups; cricket clubs, football teams, chess tournaments; the historical society, the women's institute, the museum, the hunt, the angler's club – in a thousand ways people combine not just in circles of friendship but in formal associations, willingly adopting and submitting to rules and procedures that regiment their conduct and make them accountable for doing things correctly. Such associations are a source not only of enjoyment but also of pride: they create hierarchies, offices and rules to which people willingly submit because they can see the point of them. They are also viewed with suspicion by those who believe that civil society should be directed by those who know best.

When the Communist Party took over Eastern Europe, its first work was to destroy the civil associations that it did not control.[3] János Kádár, as Minister of Home Affairs under the Rákosi government of Hungary after 1948, closed down 5,000 such associations in the course of a year: brass bands, choirs, theatre groups, boy scouts, reading societies, walking clubs, private schools, church institutions, charities for the relief of poverty, discussion societies, libraries, wine festivals, hunting and fishing clubs. Under communism, all private charity was illegal, and bank accounts set up in trust for charitable uses

---

[2] See 'The Planning Fallacy', in Roger Scruton, *The Uses of Pessimism* (London: Atlantic Books and New York: Oxford University Press, 2010).

[3] See Anne Applebaum, *Iron Curtain* (New York: Doubleday and London: Allen Lane, 2012).

were confiscated by the party. The extent of this evil is not widely known in the West, nor is its meaning often pondered. Once civil association is absorbed into the great enterprise of progress, once the future is made monarch over the present and the past, once the great goal is in place, with the state or the party leading all citizens towards it, then everything is reduced to a means, and the ends of human life retreat into privacy and darkness.

Of course, in all systems of government, it is necessary to set limits to association. Conspiracies and subversive organizations arise spontaneously even in the kindest societies, and all political orders have good reason to suppress them. Moreover, there are associations for criminal, immoral or socially destructive purposes, and the state must retain the right to control or prevent them. But it is not, as a rule, such associations that have become controversial in our societies today. If people are free to associate, then they can form long-standing institutions, outside the control of the state. These institutions might confer advantages on their members, in the form of knowledge, skills, networks of trust and goodwill. They will contribute to the stratification of society, by offering those advantages selectively. For it is a law of association that to include is to exclude; and exclusion can hurt.

Indeed, in no area does the tension between liberty and equality reveal itself more vividly than in this one. Free association leads naturally to discrimination, and the advocacy of non-discrimination leads naturally to top-down control. How do we choose the acceptable middle ground, and on whom do we confer the right to forbid us? The libertarians tell us that no one has a right to exercise this kind of control and that it will always get into the wrong hands – the hands of those who most want to herd us, in directions that we least want to go. There is a truth in that – but it is not the whole truth. For we know that our liberties are diminished if our fellow citizens are excluded from exercising them. The privileges of social membership should not be withheld from people purely on grounds – such as race or class – that are irrelevant to their exercise. For this reason, most of us now accept that where discrimination brings with it an unacceptable penalty, as in contracts of employment and admission to schools and colleges, it is part of true civil liberty to prohibit the divisive forms of it.

The question remains of the extent to which associations should be subject to this kind of control. The American Civil Rights movement ended racial segregation in America and decent people applaud the result. But the same people might be less happy to learn that the Catholic Church in Europe can no longer run adoption agencies for children in its care, since the Church's attitude to homosexual couples violates the non-discrimination clauses in European Law. They may worry that similar clauses are beginning to impact on the activities of the Boy Scouts and Church-based youth organizations, in both Europe and America.[4] Should we simply accept this, as the price of real equality? Or should we, rather, uphold the freedom to associate as we will, and as our conscience requires of us?

The problem is illustrated by the history of all-male clubs in America. Men stand in need of the 'male bonding' that enables them to make deals, to compete peacefully and to form networks of enterprise and risk-taking that fill their lives with purpose while defusing the instinct to fight. Hence they form clubs, where they meet during the evenings over drinks and food, and exchange whatever ripe or rowdy gossip takes the edge off their mutual competitiveness.

What harm in that? A great harm, say the feminists. For the club becomes an arena of privilege, a place where deals are made and careers advanced. And the deals and careers are on offer only to members and therefore only to men. Hence the male club is an instrument of unfair discrimination of a sexist kind. Only if women are admitted to the club can its existence be reconciled with the demands of social justice. As a result of this argument, all-male clubs have been made more or less illegal in America – a fairly radical assault on free association in the name of an egalitarian principle.

An equally telling example is that of the private school, and in particular the private school (called 'public') in Britain. Leaving aside the complex history of this institution, it is acknowledged on every side that the public schools, through their very autonomy, have been able to build up resources, expertise and traditions that impart not just knowledge but also style, charm and influence to the children who pass through them, and the schools offer these things selectively, to those able to afford the financial cost or clever enough to obtain a scholarship. Hence they feed into the class divisions of British society.

From time to time, egalitarians have sought to make the public schools illegal, so that all education is subsumed by the state. But the wiser among them have recognized that this will not change things very much. If you compel all children to attend state schools, then wealthier parents will compensate through

---

4   See the complex and interesting American case of *Cradle of Liberty Council* v. *City of Philadelphia*, 2008, in which the City of Philadelphia attempted to evict the Scouts from the building they had given to the city, on the grounds that the Scouts' policies on homosexuality violated the city's non-discrimination code.

private tuition, through reading at home, and through all the advantages that parents naturally and defiantly pass on to their children out of love. Plato's solution was to regard children as property of the state, to be raised in collective farms under the rule of impartial guardians. But there is a resilience in parental affection that defeats all attempts to extinguish it, and the middle classes will always manage to pass on their advantages, as they did under communism through the little platoons that I described in Chapter 2.

So what is the conservative response to this situation? One response is to argue, with some plausibility, that discrimination is unacceptable only if it is in some way unjust. And to suppose that an institution is unjust merely because it confers benefits on its members that it does not confer on others is in effect to rule out all free association and to advocate the totalitarian state. The intricate arguments that have been developed around this point – with some following Rawls, in believing that justice is fairness, others following Nozick and, ultimately, Kant, in believing that justice resides in the respect for free transactions – need not concern us. For, whether or not the existence of private schools is *in fact* unjust, many people believe it to be so. Private education is therefore the target of resentment, and resentment has to be managed, even if injustice lies in the resentment rather than its cause.

Autonomous Institutions

There is, in the circumstances of modern life, only one solution to the problem of resentment, and that is social mobility. The worst thing that the state can do is to create those traps – the poverty trap, the welfare trap, the education trap – which deprive people of the motives and the skills to improve their lot, and retain them in a state of permanent discontented dependence on a world that they cannot fully enter. In Britain, the state education system evolved from the gradual takeover by the state, during the nineteenth century, of schools established as charitable foundations, or as self-governing 'grammar' schools catering for the ambitious poor. At first the state merely provided the funding to enable these schools to offer their services free of charge. Inevitably, however, state funding led to state control, and state control to the 'politics of goals'.

I have already referred to the consequences of this (see above, Chapter 4). When the egalitarians had finished their work, the grammar schools had for the most part returned to the private sector, schools had been amalgamated in order to prevent parents from selecting among them, and the goal of equality had been imposed from above regardless of its effect on the opportunities available to the poor. The result was that Britain, which emerged from the Second World War with the best education system in the developed world, is now near the average of the OECD tables for literacy and numeracy. Positions at the top of British society continue to be occupied by those privately educated – to which egalitarians respond by calling for the closure of the private schools, so that everyone will be in the same boat. This would not change things, however. Wealthier parents would simply club together to make schools irrelevant to the prospects of their children.

Opportunities are enhanced not by closing things down, but by opening things up. It is by allowing autonomous institutions to grow, by protecting the space in which they flourish, and if necessary by providing public funds in the form of educational vouchers, that the state can enhance the opportunities available to the poorer members of society. Gradually this truth is beginning to dawn on the political class, so that even socialists have come to accept that the poor are not helped by taking revenge against the rich, but by opening the doors to social advancement. Since education has grown through autonomous institutions, we need more of those institutions, not fewer of them, and ways of ensuring that poorer people have access to them.

This means reversing the tendency of post-war legislation in the Western world. The desire to police our habits has seen the assault on autonomous institutions, from schools to adoption-agencies, from scout troops to hunts, which fail to comply with some regime of political correctness. The long-term effect of this is to absorb civil society into the state, and to subject the whole of social life to a kind of ideological vetting. The truth in conservatism is that civil society can be killed from above, but it grows from below. It grows through the associative impulse of human beings, who create civil associations that are not purpose-driven enterprises but places of freely sustained order. Politicians often try to press these associations into alien moulds, making them into instruments for external purposes that may be in conflict with their inner character. This is what happened to state schools, when they were conscripted to the pursuit of social equality. It is what happened to universities, when the pressure from governments demanded measurable results as a *quid pro quo* for funding. It is what happened to all the little platoons of Hungary, Slovakia and the Czech lands, when the Communist Party made them into 'transmission gears' for the socialist agenda.

Autonomous institutions are exactly that: institutions that follow their own internal impulses. So it is with knowledge, which lives in the institutions that transmit it as blood lives in the body, giving life and also receiving it. Although knowledge is useful, it comes about because we value it, whether or not we have a use for it, as people valued the study of the classical languages and ancient history, the study of logic and set theory, the study of probability and statistical inference. Nobody would have guessed that ten years of Latin and Greek was exactly the preparation required by those British civil servants, as they travelled around the globe to administer a multicultural empire; nobody would have foreseen that the abstruse workings of Boole's algebra and Frege's logic would lead to the era of digital technology; nobody, least of all the Rev. Thomas Bayes, had any idea of what Bayes' theorem in the calculus of probability would mean for our understanding of statistics. All such knowledge arises because people pursue it for its own sake, in the context of institutions that are maintained by our curiosity and not by our goals. The results of that curiosity may be beneficial, and governments may decide which forms of research or scholarship it would be best to fund for the sake of an acknowledged social good. But such decisions are intelligent guesses, not practical syllogisms. Astrophysics needs a lot of funding, and has produced wonderful and awe-inspiring results. Maybe it will solve the problem of climate change. But so far it has proved entirely useless, and is indeed a model illustration of the use of useless things.

The Conversational Model

Civil society, Hayek argued, is, or ought to be, a spontaneous order: an order emerging by an invisible hand from our dealings with each other. It is, or ought to be, consensual, not in the sense of issuing from some gesture of mutual consent like a contract, but in the sense of arising from voluntary transactions and the steps we take to adjust, accommodate and correct them.

One way to understand this idea is by reference to the art of conversation – an art sometimes referred to by Oakeshott as a paradigm of civil association.[5] Conversations occur between beings who are rational and who are speaking freely. They may involve two people, three, four or any number up to the limit

---

[5]   See the celebrated essay 'The Voice of Poetry in the Conversation of Mankind', in *Rationalism in Politics and Other Essays* (London: Methuen 1962), pp. 197–247.

at which the general conversation breaks down into smaller groups. But as the numbers increase, so, as a rule, does the enjoyment lessen and the potential for fragmentation grow. A general conversation among a large group of people requires discipline, rules and traditions of politeness. In the ancient world, conversations might take the form of a symposium, with one participant nominated as *archon*, whose job it was to maintain order among the participants, each of whom spoke in turn. This natural tendency of conversation towards convention, tradition and a discipline enforced from some central authority duplicates features that we observe in all forms of political order. This suggests that conversation is not, as Oakeshott sometimes seemed to imply, an *alternative* to top-down sovereignty but at best a mitigation of it, the thing that softens it from below and which also summons it.

I might speak to someone in order to give a message, to strike a bargain or to convey a command. Such speech acts fall outside the normal bounds of conversation, since they involve a goal that is prior to the act of speaking. In a normal conversation, goals emerge *from* the conversation and cannot be easily defined in advance of it. If a person talks to me in ways that make it apparent that his interest is entirely subservient to an agenda, that he has some purpose in mind that, once achieved, will bring the encounter to an end, he is not in fact *conversing*. Conversation is a form of reciprocity, in which each of us can influence and deflect the other's goals and interests, and in which no single goal governs what is said.

This does not mean that there is no distinction between a good conversation and a bad one, or that there is no measure whereby a conversation can be judged to be successful. Conversation is, as a rule, a pleasure, indeed a major source of happiness. But the good that results from conversation is a side effect and not a goal, like the exhilaration that comes from playing football, or the happiness that comes from love.

In all the respects that I have so far mentioned, conversation fits the bill of a free association which is subservient to no purpose but itself, and which is destroyed by the bossiness and urgencies of the planner, the utopian and the rationalist. On the other hand, conversations have to be among few participants if they are to dispense with some kind of central discipline or with accepted procedures and conventions. As they widen, so does the need for discipline grow. In most systems of law, therefore (Islamic law being a prominent exception), prohibitions have a far larger place than commands, and it is in terms of the breadth and intrusiveness of these prohibitions that the comparative liberality of a legal system should be measured. The point is best expressed in terms made familiar by Robert Nozick,[6] namely, that a liberal legal system is a system of side constraints. It does not fix the goals or life plans of individuals, nor does it surround them with prohibitions for which they themselves can find no reason. It simply constrains their conduct so that their goals can be pursued with the minimum of conflict, and so that, when conflict occurs, it can be peacefully resolved.

Such, surely, is what we would expect of a disciplined conversation, and it is what is implied in the concept of good manners. Furthermore, there is an interesting difference between a conversation maintained by good manners and one maintained by the top-down command of an *archon* or chairman. There is an ideal of civilization which is exemplified in the perfect seminar or dinner-table conversation, in which each person gives of his best for the others' sake, in which nobody dominates or monopolizes the theme, and in which good manners ensure that each gives way at the moment collectively required, so that the conversation can take its unpredictable course. It is rare that we encounter such a conversation, however, and it is quite clear that it can occur only between people of a certain kind – people who have internalized the rules of social intercourse, who are happy not to dominate, but who are also sufficiently good humoured to contribute as best they can.

Work and Leisure

There is another feature of conversations to which we should attend, before drawing any implications for the study of political order, and this is that they are, on the whole, the offshoots of leisure. This is surely true of those conversations that move from person to person in the manner that we might describe (borrowing from Kant) as 'purposeful without purpose'.[7] The space for such conversations must be purchased, and it is reasonable to suppose, therefore, that in modern conditions a considerable inheritance of political order is required before they can exist. Leisure exists only because people produce a surplus, and the kind of leisure that we enjoy will be marked by the kind of

---

[6] In *Anarchy, State and Utopia*, op. cit.
[7] Kant, *Critique of Judgment*, available in various translations, on the object of aesthetic interest.

work that went into creating it. In aristocratic societies those that enjoy the leisure are not those who do the work, and the delights of conversation among those esteemed 'polite' are purchased through the work of others who, on the whole, are not so.

If we are to model our political order on conversation, therefore, we need to be very clear what kind of conversation we have in mind, and what kind of work is required to produce it. In a democracy, which offers to every citizen a share in the political process, conversation must feed back into the work that purchases it. Work must not be a sphere of instrumentality and instrumental reasoning, where everything, words and relationships included, is treated merely as a means to an end. It must have the character of an end in itself, in which people can find solace and renewal of the kind that we obtain through sport, play and friendship.

In the wake of the great social and intellectual transformations that followed the Enlightenment, this matter was discussed at length by Schiller, Hegel and Marx in Germany, and by Ruskin and Morris in England. It is, in my view, a great pity that it has slipped so far down the agenda of modern political science. We surely recognize that what is sometimes called 'meaningful work' is as important an ingredient in human fulfilment as meaningful leisure. Although work is a purposeful activity, it has to be intrinsically interesting if it is to be fully acceptable to the one who engages in it.

In one of the first works of philosophy to link political order to the sphere of intrinsic values, Schiller described art as a paradigm of human fulfilment.[8] But he went further, and suggested that the pursuit of beauty through art is simply one form of a more general disposition to *enjoy* things. With the good and the useful, he wrote, man is merely in earnest; but with the beautiful he plays. And with that word he tried to link art and the aesthetic to dancing and sport, as the continuation into adult life of a blessedness that we receive as children.

The work of art, for Schiller, is *all communication*, and through it the artist speaks to the world. But few of us are artists, and most must content ourselves with lesser forms of self-expression. Moreover, a work of art succeeds when it silences those who encounter it: it is not something that you respond to by 'answering back'. For ordinary mortals, the way of self-realization through art is either unavailable or an invitation to egotism and phoniness.

---

[8] Friedrich von Schiller, *Letters on the Aesthetic Education of Mankind*, trans. E. Wilkinson and L. A. Willoughby (Oxford: Clarendon Press, 1967).

At the same time, art exemplifies at its strongest an impulse that all rational beings share: the impulse towards recognition. The artist is producing something that seeks the attention and approval of an audience. And it is undeniable that human beings spontaneously seek recognition for what they do. Dancing is mutual recognition, sport is a bid for recognition by the team, or – for the spectator – a way of identifying with that bid. Friendship is the highest form that recognition can take, when another values you for what you are, seeks your advice and company, and binds his life to yours.

The crucial point made in the wake of Schiller's argument is that this bid for recognition can occur as much in work as in play. According to Hegel, it is through recognition that the slave attains freedom, while the master loses it. Marx described work in the industrial factories as 'alienated labour'; but that which can be alienated must, by that very argument, have a normal and unalienated form. People's actions are by their nature directed to a wider world, and even if it is only their fellow workers who are in a position to judge what they do, people seek to communicate with those workers through their labour, and to elicit their approval. Teamwork achieves, at its best, a kind of mutuality of judgement that is not unlike a conversation in its ability to bring people into free relation with each other.

Human beings have only a limited amount of energy, must gird themselves to be polite and – while enjoying each other's company – cannot be always on their best behaviour. For many of them, the social intentionality that animates their work depletes the reserves that might otherwise fill their hours of leisure. Hence, for many people, communications at work are the most sustained communications that they have. In existing conditions, therefore, it is at work that the possibilities of a fulfilled and meaningful life must be exhibited. Hence the virtues of conversation must be replicated in the workplace if the conversational model of political order is to carry conviction. Work must have some of the intrinsic value that Schiller attributed to play – it must be both a bid for recognition and an expression of freedom. No more at work than in play should we be 'merely in earnest'.

Conversations may be both work-like and play-like. Both forms of conversation are expressions of freedom, both generate peace and attachment, both are intrinsically worthwhile. But the first would not exist without the shared purpose, while the second has no purpose but itself. Many people would feel suspicious of a philosophy, like Oakeshott's, that seems exclusively focused on conversation of the second kind. It seems to involve a kind of 'aestheticization' of the political sphere, and a refusal to recognize the validity of those things, like working and fighting, which create the space in which our conversations flourish. The same is true of Schiller's paradigms of art and play, and it would be true too of a political philosophy that took dancing as its model. Only if the ethos of leisure feeds back into the workplace can there be a fulfilling political order. That too should be part of Disraeli's 'feudal principle': responsive relations should inhabit all that we do, so that in work as in leisure we are in free conversation with our fellows. In the fulfilled human life, the purposeful and the purposeless should interpenetrate, so that our activities are, so far as possible, never merely instrumental, never matters of calculation alone, but always redeemed by a sense of their intrinsic value.

Friendship, Conversation and Value

Aristotle divided friendships into three kinds: friendships of utility, of pleasure and of virtue. The division applies to conversation too. There is the conversation of utility that governs a shared task, the conversation of pleasure that directs our relaxation, and the conversation of virtue that informs the bond between people who admire and cherish what they find in each other. All actual conversations involve a mixture of these things. And in taking conversation as our model of political order, we are reverting to something like Aristotle's conception of the *polis*, as a place of friendship – but without Aristotle's defence of slavery as the aspect of civil order imposed on those who are 'naturally slaves'. This suggests to me that the contrast that Oakeshott urges, between civil association and enterprise association, should be augmented by another and more radical contrast, between communities of cooperation and communities of command. Enterprise is one form of cooperation, which has its own ingress into the world of conversation, and its own role to play in the building of friendship. It is a form of free association that is governed by law, morality and good manners in just the way that leisure is governed.

The vision of the *polis* presented by Aristotle is of a society organized by and for the purpose of friendship, in which the higher friendship of virtue is encouraged, not only between individuals, but between individuals and the state. The citizen is the friend of the state, which reciprocates his friendship. Only the virtuous *polis* can be based in friendship of this kind, and the virtuous *polis* is the one that encourages virtue in its citizens.

That suggestion reminds us that the virtuous *polis* is an ideal, and that another kind of *polis* is possible, in which the friendship that binds the citizens is the friendship of utility, not virtue. And, some would have it, that better describes our position today than the noble conception put forward by Aristotle. It often seems as though modern states offer their citizens a *deal*, and that they require nothing of the citizens beyond respect for the terms of the deal. This is what Philip Bobbitt means by the 'market state': one in which the old notions of national loyalty and patriotic duty are replaced by conditional allegiance, in return for material benefits.[9] If the benefits aren't good enough, the citizen will look for them elsewhere, roaming the world in search of a better bargain. There may be conversation at the heart of the market state, but it will be like the conversation at work, predicated on a common but possibly temporary need for profit. It will be one in which deep loyalties will be withheld and attachment carefully prevented.

Aristotle's distinctions remind us that there is yet another kind of *polis*, again one depending on friendship, but this time the friendship of pleasure. Such a political order is founded neither on duty nor contract but on fun. The citizens are all part of a single fun machine, like the citizens of Huxley's *Brave New World*. Their affections are short-lived and pleasure-soaked; the tragic spirit has sunk entirely below their horizon; and loyalty to the state is purchased by the constant provision of soma. Conversation in such a world is a matter of smiles and snapshots, of brief excitements and squeals of delight. Some think that Western societies are approaching this condition, as consumption takes over from reproduction to become the high point of the human drama.

If we are to propose conversation as our model of political order, therefore, we need to answer the questions: conversation in what circumstances, between whom and of what kind? Conversations arise in human society even in the most instrumentalized of our interests and activities. And Aristotle helps us to see how the truth in conservatism morphs into another all-absorbing falsehood. Conservatives are right to emphasize free association as the root of civil society. But when free association becomes a shibboleth, when all forms of community are regarded as equally worthwhile, provided only that the participants consent to them, then we lose sight of the distinction between associations in which people make no demands of each other, and associations in which moral

---

[9]   Philip Bobbitt, *The Shield of Achilles: War and Peace in the Course of History* (New York: Alfred A. Knopf, 2002).

discipline grows between the participants and informs and transforms their lives. The truth in conservatism depends on our recognition that free association is to be valued only if it is also a source of value – in other words, only if it is ordered towards fulfilment, rather than mere utility or recreation. In the libertarian free-for-all what is worst in human nature enjoys an equal chance with what is best, and discipline is repudiated as a meddlesome intrusion. Conservatism is the attempt to affirm that discipline, and to build, in the space of free association, a lasting realm of value.

Defending Freedom

When people see their social relations in terms of utility, as in Bobbitt's market state, or as mere amusements, as in *Brave New World*, the bond of society is weakened. Societies can survive a major crisis only if they can call upon a fund of patriotic sentiment. Where that is lacking the social order crumbles at the first shock, as people scramble to secure their own safety regardless of their neighbours. So it was along the Pacific Rim when Japan launched its bid for imperial mastery, and so it was, on some accounts, in France, at the outbreak of the Second World War. It is from an awareness of this that conservatives have always emphasized the connection between a nation and its military arm. The true citizen is ready to defend his or her country in its hour of need, and sees in its military institutions an expression of the deep attachment that holds things in place.

The conservative view of political order sees the military as expressing an independently existing civil order. That was the idea contained in the old county regiments of Great Britain and Ireland, and embodied today in the American military colleges. It has its roots in Athenian democracy, which regarded military service as a duty of the citizen, to be exercised solely in defence of the *polis*, and not as a political instrument. That attitude contrasts with the Spartan idea of the military, as the expression of state power, used both to subjugate society in peacetime and to make pitiless war when the time for war has come. The totalitarian states of the twentieth century, notably Germany and the Soviet Union, exemplified the same idea, of an army that is the instrument of state power, rather than the expression of social attachment. The Nazis and communists frequently used military force against minorities within the state, often retaining, as in Germany, special troops for this purpose. The marches, the discipline and the wiped away conscience of the recruits all bore witness to this conception of the military, as the executive arm of government. Civil society was to be in awe of the military as it was in awe of the state.

Needless to say, the institutions, discipline and pageantry of military life, as the conservative conceives them, are as different from those exemplified in a military dictatorship as teamwork is different from slavery. And what is true of the military is, or ought to be, true of the police force. This too should be an expression of civil society, rooted in the local community, and responsive as much to local conditions as to the requirements of national government. So it was in the England of my youth, which was indeed world famous for the posture and ethos of its police force. Our constabulary was not an arm of central government, but a local organization, accountable to the county councils. The 'bobby' himself was trained as a friend of the community he served, and the sign of this was that he was armed only with a notebook and a comic tin whistle. He knew the people on his beat, and took a benign and paternal interest in their welfare. Children went to him when they were lost, strangers asked him directions, and everybody greeted him with a smile. Idealized, but not caricatured, in the TV series devoted to the world of PC Dixon of Dock Green, his role was to rectify wrong, to restore equilibrium, and to guide his own community along its peaceful path to nowhere. PC Dixon cultivated begonias, sang in the police choir, was a member of the police darts team and was in general as worthy a participant in the 'little platoons' of Dock Green as any of those who might be called upon to serve on the jury.

So conceived, the English police force served to emphasize a fundamental truth about the English law, which is that it exists not to control the individual but to free him. The common law is on the side of the citizen against those – whether usurping politicians or common criminals – who wish to bend him unconsenting to their will. It is that conception of law that underlies conservative politics in the English-speaking world, and it is what most stands to be defended, now, against the forces that are gathering to oppose it.[10]

---

[10] The conception has never been better defended than by a Canadian, the philosopher George Parkin Grant, *English-Speaking Justice* (Sackville, NB: Mount Allison University, 1974).

11

Realms of Value

Putting together the argument of the previous chapters, I draw the following broad conclusion: that the role of the state is, or ought to be, both less than the socialists require, and more than the classical liberals permit. The state has a goal, which is to protect civil society from its external enemies and its internal disorders. It cannot be merely the 'night watchman state' advocated by Robert Nozick, since civil society depends upon attachments that must be renewed and, in modern circumstances, these attachments cannot be renewed without the collective provision of welfare. On the other hand, the state cannot be the universal provider and regulator advocated by the egalitarians, since value and commitment emerge from autonomous associations, which flourish only if they can grow from below. Moreover, the state can redistribute wealth only if wealth is created, and wealth is created by those who expect a share in it.

The socialist obsession with distribution is a reflection not only of the 'default egalitarianism' from which democracy begins, but also of the growing materialism of our societies. This materialism informs political discourse at every level, making wealth and its distribution the only issue that is discussed for long. As a result, people think of conservatism merely as a form of complacency towards the current system of material rewards, which has nothing whatever to say about the things that 'money can't buy', or about the effect of the consumer society on our deeper values. Yet it is precisely in this area that the strength of the conservative vision lies, and in this chapter I shall try to defend the broader conception of civil society that makes conservatism, to me, so attractive.

From its beginnings in the world of the Enlightenment, conservatism has been engaged in a work of rescue. New social movements, new modes of industrial production, new political aspirations all threatened to destroy or destabilize customs, institutions and forms of life on which people in one way or another depended. And the question arose as to how those things could be protected and whether there was anything that a *politician* could do to lend support to them. Essentially the conservative is the one who answers: yes, they can be protected, but no, it is not for the politician to adopt this as a goal. All politics can do is to enlarge the space in which civil society can flourish. Value comes to us in many ways, and wherever and whenever it comes it brings with it authority, peace and a sense of membership. But it does not come through a political programme.

Nor does it come through economics. According to a famous definition given by Lionel Robbins, economics 'is the science which studies human behaviour as a relationship between ends and scarce means which have alternative uses'.[1] Economics assumes that we not only have knowledge of our ends but are also prepared to assign a price to them; and it establishes its empire over the human imagination by pricing everything that human beings might want, need, admire or value, so replacing the great questions of human life with the abracadabra of the experts. For the economist, value and price are indistinguishable and Wilde's definition of the cynic, as the 'man who knows the price of everything and the value of nothing', expresses a truth that has no translation in the dismal science. Yet those things that we truly value are precisely the things, such as life, love and knowledge, that we are reluctant to price. Value begins where calculation ends, since that which matters most to us is the thing that we will not exchange.

Moreover, our values are not given in advance of discovering them. We do not go through life with clear goals and use our reason merely to achieve them. Values *emerge* through our cooperative endeavours: those things to which we become most attached are often unforeseeable before they envelop us, like erotic love, the love of children, religious devotion, the experience of beauty. And all such things are rooted in our social nature, so that we learn to understand them and to focus upon them as ends in themselves only in dialogue with others, and seldom in advance of achieving them. Economics, which is the science of instrumental reasoning, is therefore silent about our values, and if it pretends to deal with them nevertheless it is only by putting *Homo oeconomicus* in the place that should be occupied by real human beings. Value comes about because we humans create it, and we do so through the traditions, customs and institutions that enshrine and promote our mutual accountability.

---

[1] Lionel Robbins, *An Essay on the Nature and Significance of Economic Science* (London: Macmillan, 1932), p. 16.

First among those traditions and institutions is religion, which shines a light from our social feelings far out into the unknowable cosmos. When Burke and Maistre set out to make the case against the French Revolution, they were impressed by nothing so much as its anti-religious zeal. The persecution of the Church was not just a matter of removing its social power and its property – both of which could be easily done, and had already been done two centuries earlier by Henry VIII and Thomas Cromwell in England. The Revolutionaries wanted to possess the souls that the Church had recruited, and to this end they insisted that priests swear an Oath to the Revolution, which was to take precedence over their vows of chastity and obedience. Those that refused risked death, and were hounded from one end of France to the other.

Subsequent revolutions have in like manner regarded the Church as Public Enemy number 1, precisely because it creates a realm of value and authority outside the reach of the state. It is necessary, in the revolutionary consciousness, to enter that realm and to steal its magic. Maistre believed that you could put the magic back where it belonged, restoring not just a monarchical state but the religious consensus on which it depended. Burke was less sanguine, coming as he did from a mixed background, with a Catholic mother and Protestant father, and knowing, from the case of his native Ireland, that government must hold religion at a distance if it is to maintain civil peace.

In fact, Burke foreshadowed what was to become the normal conservative position in Britain during the course of the nineteenth century. He held that an established religion, tolerant of peaceful dissent, is a part of civil society, attaching people to their home and their neighbours, and enduing their sentiments with moral certainties that they cannot easily acquire in another way; but he also recognized that it is not for the state to impose religion on the citizen or to require doctrinal conformity.

That position would, I suspect, reflect the opinion of British conservatives right up until the middle of the twentieth century. By that time, however, the secularization of society had proceeded at such a pace that talk of an 'established religion' had an all but ironical savour. The majority of British people still wrote 'C of E' on any official form requiring a statement of religious affiliation. But that did not imply that they attended an Anglican church – only that they were so far indifferent in the matter as to believe that God would not object to their pretending that they did. Meanwhile American conservatives adhered to the First Amendment to the United States Constitution, which told them that Congress should make no establishment of religion and that faith was a matter between themselves and their God. To the question 'Which God?', British people were inclined to say that it did not matter, while Americans adhered one way or another to the God of the Judaeo-Christian Bible – a God whose radical change of character between the Old Testament and the New did not particularly bother them, since it occurred before he had been called upon to deal with the far more interesting case of America.

All that is by way of asking the question, 'Where is religion, in the worldview of the modern conservative?' And the answer, I suspect, is this: religion plays an undeniable role in the life of society, introducing ideas of the sacred and the transcendental that spread their influence across all the customs and ceremonies of membership. But religious obedience is not a necessary part of citizenship, and in any conflict it is the duties of the citizen, and not those of the believer, that must prevail. It is one of the triumphs of Christian civilization to have held on to the Christian vision of human destiny, while acknowledging the priority of secular law. This was not achieved without intense conflict, and a slow, steady recognition that a society could be founded on the duties of neighbourliness and yet permit distinctions of faith. The achievement of Christian civilization is to have endowed institutions with a religious authority without demanding a *religious*, as opposed to a secular, obedience to them.

How has this been done? Christ, called upon to explain the law and how we must adhere to it, said this: 'Love the Lord thy God with all thy heart, and with all thy mind, and with all thy soul and with all thy strength; and love thy neighbour as thyself. On these two commandments hang all the law and the prophets.' In reducing the commandments to these two he was following a long-standing rabbinical tradition, which we can see at work also in the Torah, notably in the book of Leviticus, and in the teachings of Christ's contemporary, Rabbi Hillel. Christ's statement of the law was to be adopted as orthodoxy by his followers, who therefore saw the old law of prohibitions as a *deduction* from two more fundamental commandments, which do not take the form of prohibitions but of duties, and which enjoin nothing specific in the world of human affairs. The two duties command us to look on the world with a view to loving what we find, and must be obeyed inwardly before they can be translated into deeds. Exactly what deeds will follow cannot be demonstrated *a priori*, as Christ went on to show with the parable of the Good Samaritan. Approaching the world in the posture commanded by Christ, you are already open to legal innovation. Indeed, the law becomes just one among many instruments whereby we take charge of our lives and attempt to fill our hearts with the love of God, and our world with the love of our neighbour.

The story of the Good Samaritan, offered in answer to the question 'Who is my neighbour?', tells us that 'love of neighbour', while a religious duty, does not require the imposition of religious conformity, and is not a form of brotherhood. It is directed as much to the stranger as to the friend. You love your neighbour by administering to his needs in adversity, regardless of whether he belongs to you through family, faith or ethnic identity.

On this understanding, the laws that govern us do not require the kind of collective submission that the Islamists long for, and the secular order can take charge of the mutual dealings on which we all depend for survival. The point was made by Christ himself, in the parable of the Tribute Money, commanding his followers to 'render unto Caesar what is Caesar's, and to God what is God's'. Although Christianity has displayed, through its history, a full share of the intolerance that is the frequent by-product of religious faith, it is not unreasonable to perceive a constant movement towards the idea of religious freedom as a Christian duty – the duty to allow others to be what they fundamentally are, within the fold of neighbour-love. Such is 'the love to which we are commanded', as Kant described it, meaning the categorical imperative to treat the other always as an end and never as a means only. As we now understand it, with all the hindsight of our conflicted history, and with the benefit of the tradition of Christian theology reaching from St Augustine to Henri de Lubac and Karl Barth, it would be reasonable to say that, in its profound meaning, the Christian religion involves a recognition of the Other, as other than me. It is in part this that has enabled the continuous adaption of the world of faith to the world of politics. For many Christians today, the Enlightenment was the culmination of this process, the moment when Christian civilization recognized that secular law is 'ordained of God'.

It seems to me, therefore, that religious freedom is itself a legacy of the religion that has enjoyed precedence in the Western world – the faith for which the stranger and the brother have an equal claim. When that faith declines, as it has been declining during our time, there remains only the shell of the political order that grew from it. Many people hunger for the spiritual life, which that shell protected. Christianity provided that life; Islam cannot, in its present form, provide it, since it presses against the shell of secular law, and threatens always to replace it with another law entirely – a law that seeks brotherhood and shared submission, rather than neighbourhood and mutual freedom. Such a law is directed *against* the otherness of others, rather than setting out to protect it.

Christians are under an obligation to bear witness to their faith, but this does not mean inflicting their faith on other people or forcibly requiring them to adopt it. As the founder of the Christian faith showed, you bear witness not through triumphing over your rivals but through submitting to their judgement. The Christian faith, as it understands itself today, does not demand that we silence its critics, or even that we forbid them to practise their faith.

So understood, the right to bear witness is fundamental to Western civilization. Declaring our beliefs without threatening violence to those who do not share them, and without wishing to claim anything more than the space to make them known, is one of the hidden premises of citizenship as we have come to understand it. Interestingly enough, however, it is not the Islamists, but the human rights fanatics, who take greatest exception to this practice. The right to wear a cross at work, to place a cross in the classroom, to teach Christian morality in matters of sex and family life – all these have been questioned by secularists, and it is significant that the cases before the European Court of Human Rights and the Reports before the European Parliament increasingly target Christian believers, who on the whole make no threats on behalf of their faith, rather than Islamists, who recognize no human rights but only a duty of obedience.[2]

There are many American conservatives, including those influenced by the Roman Catholic tradition of natural law philosophy, who believe that, in the end, the conservative position rests on theological foundations.[3] For such people, God-given human capacities are exercised in the arts of government, and it is from these capacities that a free and law-governed civil order emerges. In this view, fundamental features of the Western democratic order are ordained of God: private property and its free exchange; accountability and the rights and duties that spring from it; autonomous institutions, in which the Holy Spirit works among us and from which we learn the ways of peace. The conservative emphasis on purposeless associations also has its theological underpinning: for it is through the renunciation of the individual will in the work of community that we learn humility and the love of neighbour.

[2]   See the cases reported by European Dignity Watch: europeandignitywatch.org (accessed 1 February 2014).
[3]   Such is the tradition of thinking explored and promoted by Russell Kirk, in and through *The Conservative Mind: From Burke to Santayana*, 1953, 7th edn (Washington, DC: Regnery, 2001), and maintained in our time by the journal *First Things*.

I suspect that if British conservatives are less disposed to think in that way this is in part because of the experience of empire, and the need to maintain civil order among people who do not share the Christian outlook. In his scathing response to the liberal individualism of John Stuart Mill, Sir James Fitzjames Stephen – who had occupied administrative and judicial positions in India – put forward a political philosophy that was deliberately purged of any specific religious belief, while nevertheless recognizing religion as an immovable part of the human psyche.[4] And I suspect that this is how most British people view the matter. We regard religion as the root of communities and a consolation in the life of the individual. But we allow it only a ceremonial role in the life of the state, which is built upon purely secular principles, including the principle of religious freedom. The realm of religious value is open to all of us: we can join churches and temples, learn the ways of holiness and righteousness, and enjoy the peace, hope and consolation that religion brings. But we must concede to others the right to be different.

This does not mean that conservatives are fully secular in their approach to civil society. On the contrary, they recognize that much that we value is marked by its religious origins. Many of the most important conservative causes involve the attempt to maintain an inheritance of consecrated things, whose aura is precious to us even if we no longer regard it as divinely bestowed. Hence conservatives are active in the defence of the countryside against the engines of progress, in the conservation of historic towns and buildings, in the defence of the forms and ceremonies of public life, and in maintaining the high culture of Europe. We depend on the realm of sacred things even without necessarily believing in its transcendental source – which is why culture matters to us.

It is true that, under the peculiar unwritten constitution of the United Kingdom, the Anglican Church has a place in government, moving in the background of political life like a faint shadow cast by some distant star. But, important though this is in moments of ceremony and civic affirmation, it no longer serves to distinguish the British from the American approach to religious freedom. We should see the ceremonial presence of the Anglican Church in our Parliament as Bagehot saw the monarchy. It is part of the 'dignified' rather than the 'efficient' aspect of government.[5] It is an inoffensive reminder of our

---

4   Sir James Fitzjames Stephen, *Liberty, Equality, Fraternity*, 2nd edn (London: Holt and Williams, 1874).
5   Walter Bagehot, *The English Constitution* (London: Chapman and Hall, 1867).

history, of where we have come from, and of the source of the moral outlook that is encapsulated in our law and customs. But it confiscates nothing from the secular culture.

As religion retreats from the public domain, moral education becomes increasingly a concern of the family, which is the seat and source of our primary attachments. The family has been regarded by everyone from St Just to Lenin as the enemy of revolutionary projects. Marx and Engels devoted a book to the demolition of the 'Holy Family', which they saw as the ideological outgrowth of property and exploitation. Attacks on the 'bourgeois family' were the stock in trade of the Sixties' radicals, and the attacks have been taken up by feminists and others in more recent times. The whole idea of sexual and reproductive norms has been dismissed as offensive by the advocates of the open lifestyle, and it is fair to say that the old-fashioned two-parent family is increasingly under threat as an institution, as people try to find other ways of living together, and other ways of bringing up children.

As with religion, however, we are dealing here with a realm of value: a forum in which people find solace in activities that have no purpose but themselves. New forms of family association may arise, old forms may decline, but still the basic truth remains that the family is a place in which the ends of life are constructed and enjoyed. It provides our primary image of home, the place that (if things go right for us) we long one day to rediscover, the treasury of feeling that we open again to children of our own. For this reason, in a secular society, conservatives have tended to be more concerned about the family and its destiny than about religion, while recognizing that the two have been, and still to some extent are, intertwined. And this has led to a certain paradox. While conceding that the family is an institution of civil society, which grows from below and reflects the elementary ties of free association, conservatives have accepted the view of the French Revolutionaries: that the state has the right to shape the family according to its own requirements.

Family law grew from the desire to protect a specific form of domestic life, based on the lifelong union of one man and one woman. But once the state became involved in tying the bonds between people, it also, in response to radical reformers, played an equal if not greater part in undoing them. Our laws against incest, bigamy and child marriage reflect the belief that marriage, as defined by the state, is to be judged in terms of another and higher standard. But when marriage is rewritten as a contract between the partners, in which future generations have no voice, those laws lose their underlying rationale. Hence, by a series of almost unnoticed changes, allowing ever easier divorce, and ever more blatant neglect of children, the state has overseen the gradual undoing of the marriage vow, to the point at which the advocacy of homosexual marriage seems not merely a logical consequence of all that has preceded it, but a manifest offer of 'equal treatment' to a previously marginalized minority.

Western society has evolved in the matter of homosexual relations, accepting that way of life, and the right of the state to endorse it through civil partnerships. But the bond between husband and wife, like that between parent and child, has a moral nature that is not to be summarized in a free agreement. Conservatives especially resonate to the old rite of passage, and wonder what business it is of the state finally to set it aside, with no clear mandate for doing so. And some are troubled by the shallow reasoning that has dominated the political discussions surrounding this move, as though the idea of equality were enough to settle every question concerning the long-term destiny of human societies.

But if we ask ourselves how it is that the advocacy of gay marriage has become an orthodoxy to which so many of our political leaders subscribe, we must surely acknowledge that intimidation has some part to play in the matter. Express the slightest hesitation on this score, and someone will accuse you of 'homophobia', while others will organize to ensure that, even if nothing else is known about your views, this at least will be notorious. Only someone with nothing to lose can venture to discuss the issue with the measure of circumspection that it invites, and politicians do not figure among the class of people with nothing to lose. Yet conservatives will recognize that the ordinary conscience will not find itself entirely at ease with a change that overthrows social norms on which people have depended throughout recorded history. In this, as in so many things, people of conservative temperament look around for the person who will speak for them, and find only an embarrassed silence. Strident minorities, acting on the growing disposition to censor their opponents, ensure that the deeper the question, the more likely it is to be settled by shallow arguments.

One Christian response is to say simply that the state can define marriage as it will, can confer whatever legal privileges on whatever couples it should single out for its protection, but that this has no bearing on the reality, which is a matter of metaphysics, not convention. Marriage, in this view, is a sacrament, and can be neither made nor unmade by the state. Nothing, therefore, is changed by the new legal order.

That response is understandable, but also short-sighted. In our secular society, the state has perforce assumed many of the functions of religion. Moreover you don't need to regard marriage as a sacrament and a vow before God in order to adhere to the traditional view of it. In every society of which records exist, marriage is seen as a bond between man and woman in which the whole of society has an interest. Marriage is the way in which families begin, and the obligations undertaken by the partners reach far beyond any contract between them to include people who are not yet born and who will depend upon the substantial tie between their parents. So it was in Roman law, which regarded marriage as a civil tie, but one that was nothing like a contract of cohabitation. As the Latin name – *matrimonium* – makes clear, the arrangement was not about sexual love but about motherhood. Husband and wife were not simply committing themselves to a life together: they were embarking on an *existential* transition, from one state of being to another, in which future children would be the most important element. This idea defined the social status of the institution, regardless of the fact that there could be sterile marriages and marriages between people past the age of child-bearing.

In tribal societies likewise, people enter a new condition through marriage. The whole tribe is involved in validating the tie between husband and wife and the wedding is a ceremonial recognition that the partners are dedicating themselves not merely to each other but to the offspring of their union and to the future of the tribe. Marriage rites celebrate both sexual union and sexual difference, conferring on the bridal couple the sacred obligation to be fruitful on behalf of the collective future, and also to produce children who will be compliant members of society.

Of course, we no longer live in tribes, and old adaptations must in turn adapt to new conditions. Even for us, however, marriage is the primary way in which social capital is transferred from one generation to the next. Even for us, marriage defines a path of sacrifice and dedication. Even for us, the bearing of children and the preparation for family life lie at the heart of the marital tie. And we experience this in the enhanced sense, during the marriage ceremony, of the otherness of the other sex, and of marriage as a 'threshold' into that sex's territory.

This does not mean that only fertile people should marry, or that there cannot be marriages that end in divorce. It means that marriage is built around a norm, which is invoked, however distantly, in all the variations that our nature and fragility demand. Take away that norm and the institution will be as though unsupported, a tent from which the central pole has been removed. It will no longer be a bond across generations with the nurture of children as its goal, but a contract for cohabitation, as temporary and defeasible as any other such deal.

Many will respond by saying that there is in any case no way back to the marital norms of previous generations. Increasingly people live alone, or pass from one temporary liaison to another, avoiding children as an unacceptable cost. And many men no longer regard the existence of children as a reason to remain in a marriage that has lost its enchantment. After all, the state is there to pick up the pieces. All this is familiar and presents a serious challenge to the conservative worldview. The whole history of marriage since the state assumed the right to create it has been a history of unsettlement. The correct response, it seems to me, is not to attempt to turn the state in another direction, so as to become the guardian of the traditional household. For this would be to concede the major point, which is that the state has the right to arrange civil society according to its own prescriptions. The correct response is to set an example, by living in another way, and by acknowledging the underlying spiritual truth, which is that marriage is a commitment made by the vows of the partners, and not by the rubber stamps of a registry office.

As for the law of marriage and the family, this must move in response to social change, but should not be the engine of change. In this area as in every other, the state exists to protect civil society, not to shape it according to some purpose that is not already implicit in the social fabric. It is only if marriage is rediscovered, as a 'substantial union' from which another and corporate personality grows, that the realm of domestic value will be returned to us. We don't know now what form the family will take in any future time. But we do know that, when it grows from the existential commitment of parents to each other and to their offspring, then it will grow as an intrinsic good, an association all of whose members can find their fulfilment and support in their mutual dealings. If the state has a role here, it is in clearing and protecting the space in which that kind of union can occur.

Religion and family are two realms of value. But the first is increasingly marginal to the lives of modern urban people, and the second is beginning to lose its privileged status, as the forum in which peace and fulfilment are to be found. For many people today, work and leisure define the primary spheres of association. And it is in these two spheres that our political visions are most seriously put to the test. The socialist conscience that burst on Western civilization during the course of the nineteenth century was less a reaction to the poverty of the new urban working class than to the nature of the work that enslaved it. There remained in the minds of both conservatives like Ruskin and radicals like William Morris the vision of another kind of labour, in which the production of goods is also the production of society, in which crafts, skills and devotion to the whole product express the freedom and self-conception of the labourer, and in which work mirrors the one engaged in it, just as the work of art mirrors the artist and the work of government frames the statesman. This romantic vision had been developed by Hegel and passed on to Marx, who both valued it as an ideal (as we see from the invocation of full communism in *The German Ideology*) and despised it as an illusion. The 'alienated labour' of the industrial process was, for Marx, a necessary stage in the process whereby capitalism would be overthrown, and the workers reunited with their human essence.

In the previous chapter I gave some credence to those half-philosophical, half-rhapsodic ideas. It is undeniable, however, that they have an antique air for us now. Industrial production is only a small fragment of a modern economy, which is devoted largely to service industries. Moreover, an ever-growing number of people are self-employed, dependent upon the networks of need and provision that abound in the modern city. At the same time, it remains true that there is a vast difference between the fulfilling and the alienating occupation, and that people are fulfilled at work only if they see their work as a realm of value – in other words, something that is as much an end as a means. Those who have a skill or a trade of their own, in which they have invested not merely time and effort but also some of their aspirations for their own life, are much more likely to be fulfilled at work than those employed in a task that they would not have undertaken, but for the money. And those who find, in their place of work, the companionship and the team spirit that reward their presence there are much more likely to go to work in a state of pleased expectancy than those who sit uncommunicative before the machine that they silently feed.

The picture painted by Marx in *Das Kapital* or by Engels in *The Condition of the Working Class in England* is now so far from the truth that some might wonder whether the nature of work is even an issue for us today. Have we not got through all that? Are we not now launched on a clear path into the future, in which the normal form of work is that of the self-employed worker, who can plug his or her skills neatly into some terminus of the information economy, and live from the juice?

For two reasons the picture is not so rosy. First, menial tasks like packaging, cleaning and waste disposal are abundant, even when the only real product of the economy is information, since they are part of maintaining and servicing the item on which that product most depends, namely people. Second, we have witnessed a de-skilling of modern societies through the loss of the technical subjects at school level and a general drift of the educational system towards the vague and the aspirational. A survey of school children conducted in the 1980s found that the top choices of career were those of teaching, finance and medicine. Children then, it seems, aimed to be socially useful and socially respected. A similar survey commissioned by Sky Television's Watch channel in 2009 delivered, as the three top career choices, sports star, pop star and actor: careers which arrive by some unpredictable turn of the wheel of fortune and which cast a spotlight on the one who pursues them without necessarily being either useful or respectable in the eyes of the rest of us.[6] Exactly how labour law and social policy should address these problems is a delicate matter. But it would surely gladden the heart of every conservative to think that unskilled or semi-skilled tasks like cleaning and waste disposal could be increasingly freed from the realm of employment and bestowed on the self-employed. A self-employed cleaner has the chance to strike up a contractual relation with his or her clients, to adjust the nature of the work to personal requirements, and to take pride in it as a personal achievement. Drudgery means doing an ungrateful task for an ungrateful person – and anyone employed at the bottom of the labour market knows what that means. The abolition of employment and its replacement by self-employment would, in my view, be a step towards overcoming the worst humiliations of menial work.

The de-skilling of society has come about in part because the educational system has changed in response to the supply rather than the demand for its product. The growth of junk degrees and phony expertise has been amplified by the availability of state funding for those who can claim a rent on the educational process. The victims of this are the students, seduced into thinking that a degree in media studies is the way to get work in the media, or a degree in peace studies a way to rectify the world. There is a great need throughout the

---

[6] See Kwasi Kwarteng et al., *Britannia Unchained: Global Lessons for Growth and Prosperity* (London: Palgrave Macmillan, 2012), Chapter 4, 'Work Ethic'. This chapter, from a book written by five young Conservative MPs, contains a striking statement of the work problem in modern Britain.

Western world for a freer system of higher education, which offers students qualifications that will be useful to them, and in which teachers have to prove their expertise. The American liberal arts college sets an example in this connection, and there is some sign that people in Europe are willing to consider setting up similar institutions, outside the control of the state and dependent for their funding only on those willing to purchase the product. This move to break a particularly tenacious state monopoly will of course be resisted. But it is happening, and the result will be not merely a reskilling of society, but a trans-formation of the workplace, as people with genuine skills take pride in their exercise, and combine with others to form the kinds of community of interest that grow through the professions.

The problem of meaningful work is not new: it had a mention in Chaucer, in Shakespeare, in Herbert, in Sterne and Fielding, long before Dickens, in *Hard Times*, puts it squarely in the centre of the picture. It is not a question that greatly bothered the Greeks, who described work as *ascholia* – the absence of leisure – meaning to imply that work was never more than a means, through which we earn the moments that really matter to us, when we expand, so to speak, into a space of our own. These moments, according to Aristotle, we devote to our higher good, which is *theoria*, or the life of the mind. And I suspect that, for many people today, it is what we do with our leisure that has become the major source of social concern. Leisure, for Aristotle, was a community-forming arena, in which we enjoy the friendships and virtues through which happiness dawns. Thanks to the internet, friendship and leisure are now very far from Aristotle's ideal. In the once normal conditions of human contact, people became friends by being in each other's presence, understanding all the many subtle signals, verbal and bodily, whereby another testifies to his character, emotions and intentions, and building affection and trust in tandem. Attention was fixed on the other's face, words and gestures. And his or her nature as an embodied person was the focus of the friendly feelings that he or she inspired. People building friendship in this way are strongly aware that they appear to the other as the other appears to them. The other's face is a mirror in which they see their own. Precisely because attention is fixed on the other, there is an opportunity for self-knowledge and self-discovery, for that expanding freedom in the presence of the other which is one of the joys of human life. The object of friendly feelings looks back at you, and freely responds to your free activity, amplifying both your awareness and his own. In short, friendship, as tradi-tionally conceived, was a route to self-knowledge.

When attention is fixed on the screen, however, there is a marked shift in emphasis. I have my finger on the button. At any moment I can turn the image off, or flick to some new encounter. The other is free in his own space, but he is not really free in mine, since he is entirely dependent on my decision to keep him there. I retain ultimate control, and in an important sense I am not risking myself in the friendship as I risk myself when I meet the other face to face. Of course, the other may so grip my attention with his messages, images and requests, that I stay glued to the screen. Nevertheless, it is a *screen* that I am glued to, and not the face that I see in it. All interaction with the other is at a distance, and can affect me only if I choose to be affected. Over this person I enjoy a power of which he himself is not really aware – since he is not aware of the extent of my desire to retain his presence in the space before me. He too, therefore, will not risk himself; he appears on the screen only on condition of retaining that ultimate control. This is something I know about him that he knows that I know – and vice versa. There grows between us a reduced-risk encounter, in which each is aware that the other is fundamentally *withheld*, sovereign within his impregnable cyber-castle. This withholding is reinforced by the known penalties of intimacy and indiscretion: the revealing remark, the expression of desire, need or tenderness will be 'all over the net', once it appears on the screen.

According to Hegel freedom involves an active engagement with the world, in which opposition is encountered and overcome, risks are taken and satisfactions weighed: it is, in short, an exercise of practical reason, in pursuit of goals whose value must justify the efforts needed to obtain them. Likewise self-consciousness, in its fully realized form, involves not merely an openness to present experience, but a sense of my own existence as an individual, with plans and projects that might be fulfilled or frustrated, and with a clear conception of what *I* am doing, for what purpose and with what hope of happiness.

All those ideas are contained in the term first introduced by Fichte, to denote the inner goal of a free personal life: *Selbstbestimmung* or self-certainty. The crucial claim of Hegel is that the life of freedom and self-certainty can only be obtained through others. I become fully myself only in contexts that compel me to recognize that I am another in others' eyes. I do not acquire my freedom and individuality and then, as it were, try them out in the world of human relations. It is only by entering that world, with its risks, conflicts and responsibilities, that I come to know myself as free, to enjoy my own perspective and individuality, and to become a fulfilled person among persons.

In his efforts to 'set Hegel on his feet', the young Marx drew an important contrast, between true freedom, that comes to us through relationship with other subjects, and the hidden enslavement that comes when our ventures outwards are not towards subjects but towards objects. In other words, he suggested, we must distinguish the realization of the self, in free relations with others, from the alienation of the self in the system of things. That is the core of his critique of private property, and it is a critique that is as much bound up with allegory and storytelling as the original Hegelian arguments. And in later writings the critique is transformed into the theory of 'fetishism', according to which people lose their freedom through making fetishes of commodities. A fetish is something that is animated by a life that is *transferred* from another source. The consumer in a capitalist society, according to Marx, transfers his life into the commodities that bewitch him, and so loses that life, becoming a slave to commodities precisely through seeing the market in goods, rather than the free interactions of people, as the place where his desires are brokered and fulfilled.

I do not endorse those critiques of property and the market, and see them as flamboyant offshoots of a philosophy which, properly understood, endorses free transactions in a market as much as it endorses free relations between people generally, indeed seeing the one as no more than an application of the other. However, the Marxist critique has direct application to the problems that we see emerging in our new world of internet addiction.

It seems to me incontrovertible that, in the sense in which freedom is a value, freedom is also an artefact, which comes into being through the mutual interaction of people. This mutual interaction is what raises us from the animal to the personal condition, enabling us to take responsibility for our lives and actions, to evaluate our goals and character, and both to understand the nature of personal fulfilment and to set about desiring and intending it. This process is crucial to the growth of the human subject, as a self-knowing agent, capable of entertaining and acting from reasons, with a developed first-person perspective and a sense of his or her reality as one subject among others. It is a process that depends upon real conflicts and real resolutions, in a shared public space where all of us are accountable for what we are and do. Anything that interferes with that process, by undermining the growth of inter-personal relations, by confiscating responsibility, or by preventing or discouraging an individual from making long-term rational choices and adopting a concrete vision of fulfilment, is an evil. It may be an unavoidable evil, but it is an evil all the same – and one that we should resist if we can.

We are rational beings, endowed with practical as well as theoretical reasoning. And our practical reasoning develops through the confrontation with risk and uncertainty. As long as we maintain a passive posture, life on the screen is risk free, and we risk nothing immediate in the way of physical danger, emotional embarrassment, or accountability to others when we click to enter some new domain. This is vividly apparent in the case of pornography – and the addictive nature of pornography is familiar to all who have to work in counselling people whom it has brought to a state of distraught dependency.[7] The porn-addict gains some of the benefits of sexual excitement, without any of the normal costs; but the costs are part of what sex means in a mature emotional life, and by avoiding them, you are undermining in yourself the capacity for real sexual attachment. This freedom from risk spreads also to other areas and is one of the most significant features of the social sites discussed earlier. You can enter and leave relationships via the screen without any embarrassment, remaining anonymous or operating under a pseudonym, and even hiding behind a false photograph of yourself. You can decide to 'kill' your screen identity at any time, and you will suffer nothing as a consequence. Why, then, trouble to enter the world of real encounters, when this easy substitute is available? And when the substitute becomes a habit, the virtues needed for the real encounter do not develop.

Risk-avoidance in human relations means the avoidance of *accountability*, the refusal to stand *judged* in another's eyes, to come *face to face* with another person, to give yourself in whatever measure to him or her, or to expose yourself to the risk of rejection. Accountability is not something we should avoid; it is something we need to learn. Without it we can never acquire either the capacity to love or the virtue of justice. Other people will remain for us merely complex devices, to be negotiated in the way that animals are negotiated, for our own advantage and without opening the possibility of mutual judgement. Justice is the ability to see the other as having a claim on you, as being a free subject just as you are, and as demanding your accountability. To acquire this virtue you must learn the habit of face-to-face encounters, in which you solicit the other's consent and cooperation rather than imposing your will. The retreat behind the screen is a way of retaining complete control of the encounter, while never

---

[7]   See Jean Bethke Elshtain, James R. Stoner and Donna M. Hughes (eds), *The Social Costs of Pornography: A Collection of Papers* (Princeton, NJ: Witherspoon Institute, 2010).

acknowledging the other's point of view. It involves setting your will outside yourself, as a feature of virtual reality, while not risking it as it must be risked, if others are truly to be met. To meet another person in his freedom is to acknowledge his sovereignty and his right: it is to recognize that the developing situation is no longer within your exclusive control, but that you are caught up by it, made real and accountable in the other's eyes by the same considerations that make him real and accountable in yours.

In sexual encounters it is surely obvious that this process of 'going out' to the other must occur, if there is to be genuine love, or if the sexual act is to be something more than the friction of body parts. Learning to 'go out' in this way is a complex moral process, which cannot be simplified without setting sex outside the process of psychological attachment. And it seems to me clear that attachment is increasingly at risk, and that the cause of this is precisely that sexual pleasure comes without justice or commitment. If we rely on the screen as the forum of personal development, we learn habits of relationship without the discipline of accountability, so that sex will be regarded in the same narcissistic way as the vicarious excitements through which it has been rehearsed. It will occur in that indefinable 'elsewhere' from which the soul takes flight, even in the moment of pleasure.

So much is at stake in the tendencies that I have described that conservatives must enter the fray at every point, exploring ways in which the new devices and new networks might be used in order to build civil society and not to undermine it. It has become too easy to use the screen to bypass the realm of value that leisure otherwise grants to us, to impede rather than to enhance the associations in which we 'come home to ourselves'. Once again, it is necessary to set an example, to show how to live in another way, so that the screen becomes a means to our real ends, rather than an unfulfilling fetish.

Unalienated leisure, the leisure that 'restores man to himself', is not a condition opposed to work or abstracted from it. It is continuous with work, a stepping back from work that also endorses work as a legitimate part of a completed life. A vision of this kind of leisure is offered in Genesis, in which we are told that God laboured for six days on the creation of the world, and on the seventh took a rest, not so as to be distracted from his work, but on the contrary so as to enjoy his achievement and to reflect on its worth. Leisure, for God, was an encounter with intrinsic value, a time to contemplate his creation and to see that it was good.

The passage from Genesis is the foundation of the Jewish respect for the Sabbath, a respect that was taken over by Christian civilization in the idea of

Sunday as a day of rest. A day of rest does not mean a vacant day. On the contrary, Sunday is also a day of rejoicing, built around an act of collective worship and a celebratory meal in which the best that can be found is offered on the family table. It is not only in the Christian and Jewish faith that this conception of the holy day has become canonical. For Muslims, the day in question is Friday, and the pagan festivals of Greece and Rome, which were the originals for the festivals of the Church, were conceived in the same way – as days of celebration and devotion, set apart from business, and imbued with a magical atmosphere of their own. This sense of apartness has been captured by Aristophanes in the *Thesmophoriazdusae*, and by the anonymous Latin author of the *Pervigilium Veneris*. It is, one might reasonably suggest, one of the universal gifts of religion, and one that has a transforming effect on the experience of leisure.

An essential component of leisure is therefore the openness to the festival. People are taken up by festivals, removed from ordinary cares, and offered a sense of the human condition as good in itself. They offer a paradigm of intrinsic value, and one to which the current complaints about leisure and its misuses do not apply. You are not, through your participation in a festival, alienated from yourself, you do not see yourself or others or the world around you in purely instrumental terms – all those grouses are as nothing, since to enter the festival is to stand in another light, to breathe another air, to be restored to your 'species being'.

The festival is a collective affirmation of a community, a rejoicing in self and other, and an outflow of gratitude to the gods. Vestiges of this survive in the American football match, in pop festivals and rodeos and of course, encrusted with materialistic excesses, in the traditional Christmas and the 'Eid al-fitr. In the festival, people rejoice in each other, look on each other with the thought 'it is good that you exist', and engage in symbolic acts which affirm the community as something higher than the individual and moreover something that is shared. (Many people noticed this at the 2012 London Olympics, in which a spirit of affirmation and charity seemed to pervade the audience and all those charged with assisting them.)

It is through festivals that we grasp the way in which we shape our social life. And they have a religious meaning. I mean 'religious' in the broadest sense of that term, to comprehend all attempts by human communities to rationalize their destiny, to reaffirm their solidarity and to acknowledge the 'real presence' among them of something higher than themselves. All true festivals point in this religious direction. And when we look on an object, be it a flower or a work of art, and see it as intrinsically worthy of our attention, we are in a measure recuperating the religious worldview, however solitary our emotion, and however far we may be from any transcendental belief.

That thought points towards yet another realm of value, which is the culture that we have built around the experience of beauty. The culture of beauty is of immense value to us, transmitting a vision of home and belonging that inspires us in our loneliest moments and which shines a light in our worst afflictions. But this realm of value has, in our time, become every bit as contested as the realms of religion and family life. I shall conclude this chapter, therefore, by sketching what I take to be the natural conservative position in the current cultural conflicts.

Just as customs emerge over time, from the countless efforts of human beings to coordinate their conduct, so do cultural traditions emerge from the discussions, allusions and comparisons with which people fill their leisure hours. A culture is a way of passing on the habit of judgement from generation to generation. This habit of judgement is vital to moral development, and is the foundation of the rites of passage whereby young people leave the state of adolescence and undertake the burdens of adult life. A healthy society therefore requires a healthy culture, and this is so, even if culture, as I define it, is the possession not of the many but of the few.

Some will be unhappy with that idea, believing either that there is no such thing as this 'judgement' to which I refer or, if there is such a thing, that it is irremediably 'subjective', with no inherent ability either to stand up to sceptical examination or to guarantee the survival of a culture in times of doubt. This response is expressed in a variety of ways and for a variety of purposes. In all its forms, however, it rests on a confusion, long ago pointed out by Kant.[8] It is true that our judgements of aesthetic objects and works of art are subjective in the sense that they issue from our personal experience, impressions and tastes. But it does not follow that they are subjective in the sense of admitting no argument in their favour, or connecting with no important experiences and emotions that might be tested by life.

Consider laughter. All rational beings laugh – and maybe only rational beings laugh. And all rational beings benefit from laughing. As a result, there has emerged a peculiar human institution – that of the joke, the repeatable

---

[8]   Kant, *The Critique of Judgement*, 1790, which puts aesthetic judgement for the first time clearly at the centre of our modern intellectual concerns.

performance in words or gestures that is designed as an object of laughter. Now there is a great difficulty in saying exactly what laughter is. It is not just a sound – not even a sound, since it can be silent. Nor is it just a thought, like the thought of some object as incongruous. It is a response *to* something, which also involves a judgement *of* that thing. Moreover, it is not an individual peculiarity, like a nervous tic or a sneeze. Laughter is an expression of amusement, and amusement is an outward-directed, socially pregnant state of mind.[9] Laughter begins as a collective condition, as when children giggle together over some absurdity. And in adulthood, amusement remains one of the ways in which human beings enjoy each other's company, become reconciled to their differences, and accept their common lot. Laughter helps us to overcome our isolation and fortifies us against despair.

That does not mean that laughter is subjective in the sense that 'anything goes', or that it is uncritical of its object. On the contrary, jokes are the object of fierce disputes, and many are dismissed as 'not funny', 'in bad taste', 'offensive', and so on. The habit of laughing at things is not detachable from the habit of judging things to be worthy of laughter.

Amusement, although a spontaneous outflow of social emotion, is also the most frequently practised form of judgement. To laugh at something is already to judge it, and when we refrain from laughing at what someone nevertheless believes to be funny, we may thereby show our disapproval of that person's stance. A joke in 'bad taste' is not just a failure: it is an offence, and one of the most important aspects of moral education is to teach children not to commit that offence. Think about this, and you will quickly see that, however difficult it may be to define such notions as 'judgement' and 'taste', they are absolutely indispensable to us.

Shakespeare provides us with a telling example of what I mean in the involved sub-plot to *Twelfth Night*. The drunken Sir Toby Belch and his disorderly companions decide to play a practical joke on Malvolio, steward to Sir Toby's beautiful cousin Olivia, in revenge for Malvolio's justified but stuck-up disapproval of their ways. The practical joke involves persuading Malvolio that Olivia loves him and will love him yet more if he obeys various absurd recommendations concerning his costume and conduct. As a result of this

---

[9] See Frank Buckley, *The Morality of Laughter* (Ann Arbor, MI: University of Michigan Press, 2003), in which the nature of laughter, as a society-forming practice among moral beings, is admirably spelled out.

prank, Malvolio is at first humiliated, then wounded, and finally locked up as mad, to be rescued at last only by the twists and turns of the somewhat farcical plot. Remorse, of a shallow kind, visits the pranksters. But the audience, which had begun by laughing with them, finds itself now looking on them with cold disdain and on Malvolio with uneasy pity. A cloud of discomfiture surrounds the play's conclusion, as the laughter that had propelled it is suddenly brought to judgement and condemned.

Those remarks do not amount to a theory of humour, or of the 'judgement of taste' on which it depends. But they point to the fact that there is nothing obscure about this judgement, which is a familiar part of everybody's life, with a vital role to play in cementing human society. Furthermore, this judgement can be educated, is in all forms morally relevant and involves many of our deepest and most important social instincts. Reflecting on amusement and humour, and their place in our lives, you get a very clear intimation of a more general truth, about the nature and meaning of culture – namely that culture is judgement, and that judgement counts.

The example also helps us to deflect what has come to be a routine dismissal of culture and the pursuit of it – a dismissal that begins from scepticism about the concept of art. A century ago, Marcel Duchamp signed a urinal, entitled it 'La Fontaine', and then exhibited it as a work of art. This famous gesture has since been repeated *ad nauseam*, and in so far as students now learn anything in art schools, it consists of the ability to perform this gesture while believing it to be original – an epistemological achievement comparable to that of the White Queen who, in her youth, could believe six impossible propositions before breakfast. One immediate result of Duchamp's joke was to precipitate an intellectual industry devoted to answering the question 'What is art?'

The literature of this industry has left a residue of scepticism that has fuelled the attack on culture. If anything can count as art, then art ceases to have a point. All that is left is the curious but unfounded fact that some people like looking at some things, others like looking at others. As for the suggestion that there is an enterprise of criticism, which searches for objective values and lasting monuments to the human spirit, this is dismissed out of hand as depending on a conception of the artwork that was washed down the drain of Duchamp's 'fountain'.

The argument has been rehearsed with malicious wit by John Carey,[10] and is fast becoming orthodoxy, not least because it seems to emancipate people

[10] John Carey, *What Good are the Arts?* (London: Faber and Faber, 2005).

from the burden of culture, telling them that all those venerable masterpieces can be ignored with impunity, that reality TV is 'as good as' Shakespeare and techno-rock the equal of Brahms, since nothing is better than anything and all claims to aesthetic value are void. However, the argument is based on the elementary mistake of thinking of art as what Mill called a 'natural kind', like water, calcium carbonate or the tiger – in other words, a kind whose essence is fixed not by human interests, but by the way things are.[11] If, in defining art, we were attempting to isolate some feature of the natural order, then our definition would certainly have failed if we could set no limits to the concept. 'Art', however, is not the name of a natural kind, but of a functional kind. The word 'art' works like the word 'table'. Anything is a table if it can be used as tables are used – to support things at which we sit to work or eat. A packing case can be a table; an old urinal can be a table; a human slave can be a table. This does not make the concept arbitrary; nor does it prevent us from distinguishing good tables from bad.

Return now to the example of jokes. It is as hard to circumscribe the class of jokes as it is the class of artworks. Anything is a joke if somebody says so. For 'joke' names a functional kind. A joke is an artefact made to amuse. It may fail to perform its function, in which case it is a joke that 'falls flat'. Or it may perform its function, but offensively, in which case it is a joke 'in bad taste'. But none of this implies that the category of jokes is arbitrary, or that there is no such thing as a distinction between good jokes and bad. Nor does it in any way suggest that there is no place for the criticism of jokes, or for the kind of moral education that has a dignified and decorous sense of humour as its goal. Indeed, the first thing you might learn, in considering jokes, is that Marcel Duchamp's urinal was one.

What I have said about jokes can be readily transferred to artworks too. Anything is art if somebody sincerely says so. For art is a functional kind. A work of art is something put forward as an object of aesthetic interest. It may fail to perform its function, in which case it is aesthetically empty. Or it may perform its function, but offensively, in which case it is brash, vulgar, obscene or whatever. But none of this implies that the category of art is arbitrary, or that there is no such thing as a distinction between good and bad art. Still less does it

---

[11] J. S. Mill, *A System of Logic*, 10th edn (London: Longmans, 1879) Book 1, Chapter 7, section 4.

suggest that there is no place for the criticism of art, or for the kind of aesthetic education that has a humane aesthetic understanding as its goal.

It is hardly surprising that jokes and artworks are so similar. For some artworks consist entirely of jokes: not just cheeky gestures like Duchamp's urinal, but also extended works of literature, like *Tristram Shandy* and *Through the Looking Glass*. Comedies and jokes appeal to the same emotional repertoire. And jokes, like works of art, can be endlessly repeatable. Still, in defining art as a functional kind I have introduced a new idea – that of 'aesthetic interest'. We are all familiar with this kind of interest, though we don't necessarily know how to define it. And we know that, like amusement, aesthetic interest is inseparable from judgement – hence the tradition of artistic and literary criticism which is one of the most striking achievements of our culture.

Works of art, like jokes, are objects of perception: it is how they look, how they sound, how they appeal to our sensory perception that matters. In aesthetic interest we see the world as it really seems: in Wallace Stevens's words, we 'Let be be finale of seem.' We then encounter a unity of experience and thought, a coming together of the sensory and the intellectual for which 'imagination' is the everyday name. This fact, which places the meaning of aesthetic experience outside the reach of science, explains its peculiar value. In the moment of beauty we encounter meaning in immediate and sensory form: we are endorsed and justified in being here, now and alive.

Aesthetic interest is an interest in appearances. But there are appearances that we ought to avoid, however much they fascinate us. By contrast, there are appearances which are not merely permissible objects of aesthetic interest, but which reward that interest with knowledge, understanding and emotional uplift. We deplore the Roman games, at which animals are slaughtered, prisoners crucified and innocents tormented, all for the sake of the spectacle and its gruesome meaning. And we would deplore it, even if the suffering were simulated, as in some cinematic replication, if we thought that the interest of the observer were merely one of gleeful fascination. But we praise the Greek tragedy, in which profound myths are enacted in lofty verse, in which the imagined deaths take place out of sight and unrelished by the audience. An interest in the one, we suppose, is depraved; in the other, noble. And a high culture aims, or ought to aim, at preserving and enhancing experiences of the second kind, in which human life is raised to a higher level – the level of ethical reflection.

A culture does not comprise works of art only, nor is it directed solely to aesthetic interests. It is the sphere of *intrinsically interesting artefacts*, linked by the faculty of judgement to our aspirations and ideals. We appreciate jokes, works of art, arguments, works of history and literature, manners, dress, rituals and forms of behaviour. And all these things are shaped through judgement. A culture consists of all those activities and artefacts that are organized by the 'common pursuit of true judgement', as T. S. Eliot once put it.[12] True judgement involves the search for meaning through the reflective encounter with things made, composed and written with such an end in view. Some of those things will be works of art, addressed to the aesthetic interest; others will be discursive works of history or philosophy, addressed to the interest in ideas. Both kinds of work explore the meaning of the world and the life of society. And the purpose of both is to stimulate the judgements through which we understand each other and ourselves.

Artistic and philosophical traditions therefore provide our paradigm of culture. And the principle that organizes a tradition also discriminates within it, creating the canon of masterpieces, the received monuments, the 'touchstones' as Matthew Arnold once called them, which it is the goal of humane education to appreciate and to understand.[13] Hence the conservative defence of realms of value will focus on the curriculum, and on keeping present in the minds of the young those great works that created the emotional world in which they live, whether or not they are yet aware of it.

Fundamental to that enterprise is the love of beauty. Philosophers of the Enlightenment saw beauty as a way in which lasting moral and spiritual conceptions acquire sensuous form. And no romantic painter, musician or writer would have denied that beauty was the true subject matter of art. But at some time during the aftermath of modernism, beauty ceased to receive those tributes. Art increasingly aimed to disturb, subvert or transgress moral certainties and it was not beauty but originality – however achieved and at whatever moral cost – that won the prizes. Indeed, there arose a widespread suspicion of beauty, as next in line to *kitsch* – something too sweet and inoffensive to be pursued by the serious modern artist. In a seminal essay – 'Avant-garde and kitsch', which appeared in the *Partisan Review* in 1939 – the critic Clement Greenberg starkly contrasted the avant-garde of his day with the figurative painting that competed with it, dismissing the latter (not just Norman Rockwell, but greats like Edward Hopper) as derivative and without lasting significance. The avant-garde, for

[12] T. S. Eliot, *On the Use of Poetry and the Use of Criticism* (London: Faber, 1933).
[13] Matthew Arnold, *Culture and Anarchy* (London: Smith, Elder and Co., 1869).

Greenberg, promoted the disturbing and the provocative over the soothing and the decorative, and that was why we should admire it.

The value of abstract art, Greenberg claimed, lies not in beauty but in *expression*. The emphasis on expression is a legacy of the Romantic movement; but it went with the conviction that the artist is now outside bourgeois society, defined in opposition to it, so that artistic self-expression is also a transgression of ordinary moral norms. We find this posture overtly adopted in the art of Austria and Germany between the wars – for example, in the paintings and drawings of Georg Grosz, in Berg's *Lulu* (a loving portrait of a woman whose only discernible goal is moral chaos) and in the seedy novels of Heinrich Mann. And the cult of transgression is a leading theme of the post-war literature of France – from the writings of Georges Bataille, Jean Genet and Jean-Paul Sartre to the bleak emptiness of the *nouveau roman*.

There have been great artists who have tried to rescue beauty from the perceived disruption of modern society – as T. S. Eliot tried to recompose, in *Four Quartets,* the fragments he had grieved over in *The Waste Land*. And there were others, particularly in America, who refused to see the sordid and the transgressive as the *truth* of the modern world. For artists like Edward Hopper, Samuel Barber and Wallace Stevens, ostentatious transgression was mere senti-mentality, a cheap way to stimulate an audience and a betrayal of the sacred task of art, which is to magnify life as it is and to reveal its beauty – as Stevens reveals the beauty of 'An Ordinary Evening in New Haven' and Barber that of 'Knoxville, Summer of 1915'. But somehow those great life-affirmers lost their position at the forefront of modern culture.

So far as the critics and the wider culture were concerned, the pursuit of beauty was increasingly pushed to the margins of the artistic enterprise. Qualities like disruptiveness and immorality that previously signified aesthetic failure became marks of success; while the pursuit of beauty was regarded as a retreat from the real task of artistic creation, which is to challenge orthodoxy and to break free from conventional constraints. This process has been so normalized as to become a critical orthodoxy, prompting Arthur Danto in his Paul Carus lectures to argue that beauty is both deceptive as a goal and in some way antipathetic to the mission of modern art.[14] Art has acquired another status, and another social role.

Indeed, it might seem that, wherever beauty lies in wait for us, there arises

[14] Arthur Danto, *The Abuse of Beauty* (Chicago and La Salle, IL: Open Court, 2003).

a desire to pre-empt its appeal, to smother it with scenes of destruction. Hence the many works of contemporary art which rely on shocks administered to our failing faith in human nature – such as the crucifix pickled in urine, by Antonio Serra. Hence the scenes of cannibalism, dismemberment and meaningless pain with which contemporary cinema abounds, with directors like Quentin Tarantino having little else in their emotional repertoire. Hence the invasion of pop music by words and rhythms that speak of unremitting violence, often rejecting melody, harmony and every other device that might make a bridge to the old world of song. And hence the music video, which has become an art form in itself, devoted to concentrating into the time span of a pop song some startling new account of moral chaos.

Those phenomena record a habit of desecration, in which life is not so much celebrated by art as *targeted* by it. Artists are now able to make their reputation by constructing an original frame, in which to put the human face on display and throw trash at it. What do we make of this, and how do we find the way back to the thing that so many people long for, which is the vision of beauty? Maybe it sounds a little sentimental to speak in that way of a 'vision of beauty'. But what I mean is not some saccharine, Christmas-card image of human life, but rather the elementary ways in which ideals and decencies enter our ordinary world and make themselves known, as love and charity make themselves known in Mozart's music. There is a great hunger for beauty in our world, and it is a hunger that popular art often fails to recognize and much serious art defies.

It is only because there are artists, writers and composers who have, through the last half-century of negativity, devoted their labours to keeping beauty alive that we can hope to emerge, one day, from the tedious culture of transgression. We should surely greet as heroes of our time writers like Saul Bellow and Seamus Heaney, composers like Henri Dutilleux and Michael Tippett, and architects like John Simpson and Quinlan Terry, who have kept beauty in place, allowing it to shine above our troubled world and to point a way in our darkness. Whatever their politics, those artists are the true conservatives of our time, since they have recognized that there can be no artistic truth without the tradition that makes it possible, and have devoted their creative lives to maintaining, adapting and transforming that tradition, so that it does not die.

In the eighteenth century, when organized religion and ceremonial kingship were losing their authority in the minds of thinking people, when the democratic spirit was questioning inherited institutions, and when the idea was abroad that it is not God but man who makes laws for the human world, the idea of the sacred suffered an eclipse. It seemed, to the thinkers of the Enlightenment, little more than a superstition, to believe that artefacts, buildings, places and ceremonies could possess a sacred character, when all of these things were the products of human design. The idea that the divine reveals itself in our world, and seeks our worship, seemed both implausible in itself and also incompatible with science.

At the same time, philosophers like Shaftesbury, Burke, Adam Smith and Kant recognized that we do not look on the world only with the eyes of science. There is another attitude – one not of scientific enquiry, but of disinterested contemplation – which we direct towards our world in search of its meaning. When we take this attitude we set our interests aside; we are no longer occupied with the goals and projects that propel us through time; we are no longer engaged in explaining things or enhancing our power. We are letting the world present itself and taking comfort in its presentation. This is the origin of the experience of beauty. There may be no way of accounting for that experience as part of our ordinary search for power and knowledge. It may be impossible to assimilate it to the day-to-day uses of our faculties. But it is an experience that self-evidently exists, and which is of the greatest value to those who receive it.

The haste and disorder of modern life, the alienating forms of modern architecture, the noise and spoliation of modern industry – these things have made the pure encounter with beauty a rarer, more fragile and more unpredictable thing for us. Still, we all know what it is, suddenly to be transported by the things we see, from the ordinary world of our appetites to the illuminated sphere of contemplation. It happens often during childhood, though it is seldom interpreted then. It happens during adolescence, when it lends itself to our erotic longings. And it happens in a subdued way in adult life, secretly shaping our life projects, holding out to us an image of harmony that we pursue through holidays, through homebuilding and through our private dreams. We are needy creatures, and our greatest need is for home – the place where we find protection and love. We achieve this home through representations of our own belonging. We achieve it not alone but with others. And all our attempts to make our surroundings look right – through decorating, arranging, creating – are attempts to extend a welcome to ourselves and to those whom we love. Hence our human need for beauty is not simply a redundant addition to the list of human appetites. It is not something that we could lack and still be fulfilled as people. It is a need arising from our metaphysical condition, as free individuals, seeking our place in an objective world. We can wander through this world, alienated, resentful, full of suspicion and distrust. Or we can find our home here, coming to rest in harmony with others and with ourselves. And the experience of beauty guides us along this second path: it tells us that we *are* at home in the world, that the world is already ordered in our perceptions as a place fit for the lives of beings like us.

Look at any picture by one of the great landscape painters – Poussin, Guardi, Turner, Corot, Cézanne – and you will see that idea of beauty celebrated and fixed in images. It is not that those painters are turning a blind eye to suffering, or to the vastness and threatening quality of the universe, of which we occupy so small a corner. Far from it. Landscape painters show us death and decay in the very heart of things: the light on their hills is a fading light; the walls of their houses are patched and crumbling like the stucco on the villages of Guardi. But their images point to the joy that lies incipient in decay, and to the eternal that is implied in the transient.

For the most part, our lives are organized by transitory purposes: the day-to-day concerns of economic reasoning, the small-scale pursuit of power and comfort, the need for leisure and pleasure. But little of this is memorable or moving to us. Every now and then, however, we are jolted out of our complacency, and feel ourselves to be in the presence of something vastly more significant than our present interests and desires. We sense the reality of something precious and mysterious, which reaches out to us with a claim that is in some way not of this world. That is the experience of beauty. There is absolutely nothing to be gained from the kind of insults hurled at this experience by those who cannot bear to look the mystery of our condition in the face. There is a lesson contained in the culture of desecration: in attempting to show us that our human ideals are worthless, it shows *itself* to be worthless. And when something shows itself to be worthless, it is time to throw it away.

For the conservative it is therefore plain that nothing is achieved by the culture of transgression save the loss that it revels in – the loss of beauty, as a value and a goal. To mount a full riposte to the habit of desecration we need to rediscover the affirmation and the truth to life without which artistic beauty cannot be realized. As the early modernists show, this is no easy task. If we look at the true apostles of beauty in our time, we are immediately struck by the immense hard work, the studious isolation and the attention to detail that has characterized their craft. In art, beauty has to be *won*, and the work is always harder, as the sheer noise of desecration – amplified now by the internet – drowns out the still small voice of our humanity.

One response is to look for beauty in its other and more everyday forms – the beauty of settled streets and cheerful faces, of natural forms and genial landscapes. It is possible to return to ordinary things in the spirit of Wallace Stevens and Samuel Barber – to show that we are at home with them, and that they magnify and vindicate our life. Such is the overgrown path that the early modernists cleared for us. There is no reason yet to think that we cannot clear it again. And in the spheres of architecture, town planning and the conservation of the countryside, the lamp of beauty still shines before us.

I have briefly reviewed the realms of value where conservatives have a case to make, and where their making the case will serve the greater good of the community. It is not a political case, but a case that invites us to live in another way, and in accordance with other lights and examples. But that is the way in which the life of civil society is mended, and it is only the continuing shadow cast by socialism in the minds of modern people that leads them to think that these matters can be addressed or rectified through exerting powers that belong to the state. Of course the state needs a cultural policy, since legislation impacts in a multitude of ways on the world of leisure. And this policy must be informed by judgement – not lending support to the habits of desecration and dumbing down, but responding to the true voice of our culture. But that voice is not in itself a political voice, and will be heard only if conservatives are active in creating and defending the realms of value that I have described in this chapter.

12

Practical Matters

Always there will be the cry for another kind of attachment than that arising from free association and civil society. Always there will be those who see political life as the opportunity for mass movements of solidarity, perhaps with themselves in charge. In *The Uses of Pessimism* I have attempted to expose the fallacies to which that attitude leads. I see mass movements of solidarity as arising when the stock of reason gives out – they are the place to which we return when we cease to negotiate, cease to recognize the other as entitled to his otherness, cease to live by the rule of humility and compromise. Mass movements reflect the default position of the human psyche, when fear, resentment or anger take over, and when no social order seems acceptable without an absolute unity of purpose.

Constantly in the Old Testament we see this default position showing through the rags of civil order, with the Lord of Hosts often joining in the work of destruction, and the prophets fulminating on his behalf. And we see it in the revolutions of modern times, not least in those of the communists and fascists. We find it in the language of Marx and Lenin – the secular prophets who speak for the god of 'history', who is to triumph over all our idols. This prophetic language rises like a mist from the pool of our inner resentments. Conservatives understand this; they wish to keep the frail crust of civilization in place as long as possible, knowing that beneath it there does not lie the idyllic realm of Rousseau's noble savage, but only the violent world of the hunter-gatherer. Faced with civilizational decline, therefore, they hold with Lord Salisbury that 'delay is life'.

My argument has implied that the virtues of the Western democracies are inseparable from the secular rule of law, and that secular law is inherently territorial. Only such a law can accommodate differences of religion, lifestyle and ethnicity under a shared form of civil obedience. Hence we are committed to the nation state, and the continuing attempt by trans-national bodies to confiscate the legislative powers of sovereign nations must be resisted. Some say that, in the case of Europe, this is a lost cause. But that is only because our political class has refused to act on the opportunities available, seeing the advantages to itself in the ability to pass all difficult questions to a committee of unaccountable bureaucrats, housed in some spectral tower of glass in the dispossessed city of Brussels.

There is another reason, too, why our politicians have succumbed to the bureaucrats in this matter, and that is the rise and triumph of economics, and its transformation from the science of instrumental reasoning to the ideology of modern life. As a science, with its roots in decision theory, economics involves the valid application to everyday life of indisputable mathematical theorems. As an ideology, however, describing the behaviour of *Homo oeconomicus*, it involves the *replacement* of everyday life by a more manageable caricature. As I suggested in the previous chapter, conceived as an ideology, economics describes a world in which value is given in advance of our associations, in which the goals of life are clear and predetermined, and in which the task of politics is simply to assess the costs and benefits and choose the 'optimal' solution. When economics triumphs over politics, the sole 'experts' consulted are those who promise to replace the difficult, because human, questions of political choice with the easy, because mathematical, questions of economics, starting from assumptions that no one would ever make were he not in the grip of a self-aggrandizing obsession.

Imagine a family, wondering how best to budget for the year ahead. There is a mother who does not work, because she wants to be with her children, one of whom is disabled. There is a father who is a qualified electrician, but who prefers his job teaching physics in the local school. They have a house in a beautiful place, surrounded by a plot of land that secures their view. And they carefully allocate resources so as to retain the best that life has offered them so far, which is their affection for each other, their neat home, and the routines of a life that has sufficed to keep them happily together. Their budget is planned in such a way as to enhance those things. The mother decides to work part-time from home as secretary to a postal sales firm; the father puts aside time to offer his services as an electrician to the neighbours; the children are encouraged in directions that reconcile their attachment to home with some rewarding occupation. In all this there are certain givens, which are the values that have arisen through their being together in the same place and with the interlocking attachments that have arisen there.

The economist, surveying their situation, will be appalled that they have considered only the tiniest part of their economic problem. Look at all the factors that they have not entered into the equation: their house, which could be exchanged for another at a considerable profit; their land, on which they could build three or four bungalows for rent or sale; the father's occupation, which could be exchanged for a far more profitable job as an electrician; the mother's time with her children, likewise; the disabled child, who could be placed in a home where he would be better cared for than by his mother, freeing her for productive work. Indeed, the economist would say, that is only the beginning. We could move the entire family into another and smaller house, and replace them with a collection of younger people brought from elsewhere, who would boost the productivity of this little piece of earth, and fully compensate the family with the rent. An old and tired piece of England would be renewed, and the occupants would be better off, living from the new surplus produced by the incomers, and able to pursue new and productive careers made possible by the revitalization of their local economy.

That is the way in which the case for Europe has been argued, by those who have failed to understand that *oikonomia* without the *oikos* ceases to be a practical science and becomes an ideology instead, an ideology every bit as insane as Marxism or fascism. The old guard of the Tory Party, who conspired to rid it of Margaret Thatcher, did so on the grounds that she refused to follow this way of thinking. Now the Liberal Democrats are repeating their arguments, insisting that the British economy will suffer if we do not continue to replace our workforce with recruits from elsewhere, and regarding with indifference the fact that so many of our inner city schools are filling with children who do not speak English. Indeed, this change is welcomed as a sign that economic thinking has triumphed over the benighted forms of attachment dear to 'Little Englanders'.

There is a real question for conservatives as to how this political class, so seemingly detached from ordinary loyalties, came into being.[1] In the case of leftists, the mystery is not so difficult to unravel. There are avenues into politics on the left that bypass all natural forms of human life. You start with a cause, you join an NGO (a non-governmental organization), try to squeeze into a quango, enter local government, acquire the habit of dispensing other people's

---

[1] For a brief discussion of this question, in relation to America, see Angelo M. Codevilla, *The Ruling Class* (New York: Beaufort Books, 2010).

money, and learn to play the political machine. All that can be achieved without risk and without ever doing what others would regard as an honest day's work.

To some extent there are such avenues into politics on the right too: you start with a kind of polished moral emptiness and present yourself as a consultant – in other words, someone for whom no business had a need until you came along to invent it. Almost all modern businesses are encrusted with these barnacles – management consultants, PR consultants, consultants in 'corporate social responsibility', and so on, busy reminding the directors of problems that would never otherwise have occurred to them. And there are ways into conservative politics from there, since it is the business of consultants to lobby on their clients' behalf. Still, it is not necessary that this process should yield a political class as detached from humanity as the one we see. There ought to be ways in which a consultant every now and then brushes against reality, so as to understand that we live through our attachments and are lost when they are taken away.

On both left and right, politicians have assumed the habit of avoiding or overriding the concerns of the electorate, in order to make public display of their celebrity status. This has come about in both Europe and America, and is only marginally encouraged by the EU, useful though that has proved in allowing British politicians to say, in the face of every serious question, that it is 'out of our hands'. The influence of the 'fourth estate', as Burke called the media of his day, is unavoidable; but it seems that politicians no longer have a settled will to resist it, and are prepared to put their media image ahead of the national interest in any contest between them.

It is partly because of this that the question of immigration has become politically contentious, even in those countries, such as the USA and Australia, which have retained control over their borders. For immigration is an issue in which liberal journalists can put their consciences on cost-free display, and thereby posture as the champions of the vulnerable. There is constant pressure in America to offer an amnesty to illegal immigrants – in other words, to accept as citizens people who have shown their contempt for the law. In the case of Britain, matters have gone much further, the Labour Party having encouraged mass immigration regardless of quantity or quality, and the European Treaty having in any case cancelled national sovereignty over this, the single most important issue in British politics. So important has the issue become, indeed, that it is precarious now to discuss it, for fear of the witch-hunts and persecutions that will inevitably follow.

Hence there is another cause that must urgently be fought for, and that is freedom of speech. Modern methods of censorship do not, on the whole, involve the state – although the emergence of hate crimes in European jurisdictions is a disturbing indication of the direction in which things are going. For the most part, censorship is now exercised by intimidation.

In the matter I have just referred to – the matter of protecting the integrity of civil society in the face of otherwise uncontrolled immigration – it has been for a long time the case that the conservative voice can speak only in whispers if it is not to attract the censor. Likewise in any matter that might lead to criticism of habits associated with militant Islam, we encounter intimidation of a kind unknown in Britain since the seventeenth century. Even in America a mealy-mouthed deference is adopted in matters where Islamists have staked a claim to political territory, or where the malign effect of their religious beliefs might be part of the problem.

The freedom to entertain and express opinions, however offensive to others, has been regarded since Locke as the *sine qua non* of a free society. This freedom was enshrined in the American Constitution, defended in the face of the Victorian moralists by John Stuart Mill, and upheld in our time by the dissidents under communist and fascist dictatorships. So much of a shibboleth has it become, that commentators barely distinguish free speech from democracy, and regard both as the default positions of humanity – the positions to which we return if all oppressive powers are removed from us. It seems not to occur to people now that orthodoxy, conformity and the hounding of the dissident define the default position of mankind, or that there is no reason to think that democracies are any different in this respect from Islamic theocracies or one-party totalitarian states.

Of course, the opinions that are suppressed change from one form of society to another, as do the methods of suppression. But we should be clear that to guarantee freedom of opinion goes to a certain extent against the grain of social life, and requires people to take risks that they may be reluctant to take. For in criticizing orthodoxy you are not just questioning a belief; you are threatening the social order that has been built on it. Moreover, orthodoxies are the more fiercely protected the more vulnerable they are.

Both those principles are surely obvious from the reaction of Islamists to criticisms directed at their religion. It is precisely what is most absurd that is most protected, just as it was in the wars of religion that ravaged Europe in the seventeenth century. And the critic is not treated merely as a person with an intellectual difficulty: he is a threat, the enemy of society and of God. It is not surprising therefore to find Islamists in the forefront of modern censorship.

Of course, we say to ourselves, the Enlightenment freed us from all of that. There are no protected orthodoxies in Western societies, and no one need suffer for opposing them. So here are two to think about: (1) There are no relevant differences between men and women when it comes to matters of employment, aptitude, or the tenure of office; (2) All cultures are equal, and none has a special claim to legal or political precedence. Those two orthodoxies are being enshrined in the laws handed down by the European Commission and the European Courts. Readers can probably think of people who have been hounded for denying one or other of them. Prominent among the persecutors are the humanists, the secularists and the advocates of human rights, for many of whom it is outrageous that people with unorthodox views should hold positions of influence.

Conservatives should not need reminding of this. As a rule, their views are not *criticized* but *held against them* in any question of public office or academic preferment. Over the last two decades a social order has been built on leftist doctrines, and the age-old fear of the heretic is aroused by anybody who shows even the slightest reservations as to whether those doctrines are true. Heresy is not to be argued with, but to be stamped out. Locke's essay on Toleration of 1689 argued for the toleration of opinions and ways of life with which you do not agree, as one of the virtues of a liberal society. But many who call themselves liberal today seem to have little understanding of what this virtue really is. Toleration does not mean renouncing all opinions that others might find offensive. It does not mean an easy-going relativism or a belief that 'anything goes'. On the contrary, it means accepting the right of others to think and act in ways of which you disapprove. It means being prepared to protect people from negative discrimination even when you hate what they think and what they feel. But self-declared liberals today will campaign to exclude people from office or from public speaking on account of their unorthodox opinions. Currently the iconic issue is homosexuality, which has replaced fox-hunting and immigration as the test of what is socially acceptable at the Islington dinner table. Tomorrow the totemic issue could be Christianity, incest or even (as in Huxley's *Brave New World*) motherhood. What matters is not the particular doctrine, but the refusal to tolerate dissent from it.

Toleration means being prepared to accept opinions that you intensely dislike. Likewise democracy means consenting to be governed by people whom you intensely dislike. This is possible only if we retain our trust in negotiation and in the sincere desire, among politicians, to compromise with their opponents. Hence in both Britain and America it is necessary for conservatives to defend the politics of compromise, and to protect all those institutions and customs that give a voice to opposition. This is more important than the democratic process itself, since it is the precondition of any kind of political order that responds to movements from below, and which can call the government to account.

Increasingly, however, we have seen the attempt by governments to make laws that will be irreversible, which will fatally tie the hands of the opposition or which are pushed through the legislature without due respect for the many counter-vailing arguments or the real and perceived interests of minorities. The creation of a Scottish Parliament, in which the English had no say, and which has given two votes to the Scots – one to govern themselves and one to govern the English – is one instance of the kind of gerrymandering that now regularly occurs in British politics. As a result of this move, the Labour Party hoped to rely on a block vote of virtually unaccountable Labour Members in Westminster – unaccountable because those who elect them are independently represented in the Scottish Parliament, and therefore have little need to take their pressing concerns to Westminster. Failing the creation of an English Parliament, nothing short of Scottish independence will enable the English, who have voted Conservative in 8 out of 11 post-war elections, to have the government they vote for.

In America, too, there has been a notable polarization of politics in recent decades, and an attempt to use the executive power in order to make the policies of a temporary presidential incumbent irreversible. The abuse of the Supreme Court is notorious, with sly and subtle jurists providing arguments that decide issues in ways that the elected Congress rejects, while claiming that they have the authority of a Constitution to which all are bound to adhere. In effect, the Constitution has been used by both major parties to override opposition. If you make some matter into a constitutional issue, then it can be decided by the elite and without regard for the people as a whole. The overriding of the British Parliament by the EU legislative and judicial machine has its equivalent in the overriding of Congress by the Supreme Court, the only difference being that, in the American case, the winning side represents a force internal to the nation, rather than a bureaucracy purporting to represent a federation of foreign powers. In neither case, however, are the limits defined.

Those issues reflect the role of government in protecting civil society from invasion and individuals from intimidation and violence. But in the other matters I have discussed – notably the health of civil society and its ability to grow from below – the main emphasis of conservative politics ought now to be in freeing autonomous associations from adverse regulation. In this connection no cause is more important, I believe, than that of education, which needs to be steadily liberated from the state and given back to society. The freedom of citizens to establish schools of their own, to recruit teachers with genuine knowledge and to make free and enforceable deals with parents is one that the British Conservative Party has come round to supporting. In America it took the Home Schooling movement, led by the Amish, to establish that ordinary people have a constitutional right to reclaim their children from the state. And the Labour Party in Britain is determined to resist all measures that give to parents the freedom to slip unnoticed from the system. But, if the argument of the previous chapter is right, there is no more necessary reform from the conservative point of view, since it is the reform that will allow the most important of our autonomous institutions – those concerned with the handing on of our inheritance – to avoid being captured by their enemies.

13

A *Valediction Forbidding Mourning, but Admitting Loss*

We tell ourselves comforting stories about the innocence of former times, and cherish the ambition to curl up in the past – but a doctored past, from which the grim bits have been carefully excised. And then, when we wake up, we mourn the loss of a dream.

We should not resist this tendency entirely. In particular, we should acknowledge our losses, the better to bear them. I think this is especially true of the loss of religion. Romantic and post-Romantic thinkers have looked on the world of faith from a point of view outside it, and listened, with Matthew Arnold, to that

> ... melancholy, long, withdrawing roar,
> Retreating, to the breath
> Of the night-wind, down the vast edges drear
> And naked shingles of the world.

And they have felt, as Arnold did, a sudden chill of apprehension, a recognition that something vital is about to disappear, and that in place of it there will be a troubled emptiness.

Arnold wrote 'Dover Beach' in 1867, and his reflections on the dwindling of the Christian faith are marked by a very English melancholy, a not-quite-resigned attempt to fit the world of unbelief and scientific scepticism into the Gothic frame of Anglican culture. Twenty years later, Nietzsche, in *Human, All-Too-Human*, while ostensibly throwing in his lot with the scientific atheists, recognized the enormous moral trauma that our civilization must undergo, as the Christian faith recedes. Faith is not simply an addition to our repertoire of ordinary opinions. It is a transforming state of mind, a stance towards the world, rooted in our social nature and altering all our perceptions, emotions and beliefs.

The distinction between Arnold and Nietzsche is the distinction between two kinds of loss. Arnold's loss of faith occurs in a world made by faith, in which all the outer trappings of a religious community remain in place. Nietzsche's loss of faith is an absolute loss, not only a loss of inward conviction but also of the outward symbols of faith, which for Nietzsche were mere sentimental baubles. Nietzsche is foreseeing a new world, in which human institutions will no longer be shored up by pious habits and holy doctrines, but rebuilt from the raw, untempered fabric of the will to power. Loss of faith for Arnold is a personal tragedy, to be regretted but concealed. Loss of faith for Nietzsche is an existential transfiguration, to be accepted and affirmed, since the world no longer permits an alternative. The contrast between these two attitudes can be witnessed today, with the scientific optimists joining Nietzsche in welcoming our liberation from the chains of dogma, and the cultural pessimists joining Arnold in his subdued lamentation.

Whatever our own position, we should acknowledge Arnold's foresight in predicting something that Nietzsche hid from himself, namely:

> ... a darkling plain
> Swept with confused alarms of struggle and flight,
> Where ignorant armies clash by night.

That is surely an accurate prophecy of the godless century that was to follow. Nietzsche wrote at a time when doubt and scepticism were still a kind of luxury, and when unbelief had not spread far beyond the heads of seriously educated people. In retrospect, his adulation of the 'free spirit', the *Übermensch* and the will to power show a blindness to what might happen, should these things get into heads less intelligent than his own.

A religion is not something that occurs to you; nor does it emerge as the conclusion of an empirical investigation or an intellectual argument. It is something that you join, to which you are converted, or into which you are born. Losing the Christian faith is not merely a matter of doubting the existence of God, or the incarnation, or the redemption purchased on the Cross. It involves falling out of communion, ceasing to be 'members in Christ', as St Paul puts it, losing a primary experience of home. All religions are alike in this, and it is why they are so harsh on heretics: for heretics pretend to the benefits of membership, while belonging to other communities in other ways.

This is not to say that there is nothing more to religion than the bond of membership. There is also doctrine, ritual, worship and prayer. There is the vision of God the creator, and the search for signs and revelations of the transcendental. There is the sense of the sacred, the sacrosanct, the sacramental and the sacrilegious. And in many cases there is also hope for the life to come. All those grow from the experience of social membership and also amend it, so that a religious community furnishes itself with an all-embracing *Weltanschauung*, together with rituals and ceremonies that affirm its existence as a social organism, and lay claim to its place in the world.

Faith is not therefore content with the cosy customs and necromantic rites of the household gods. It strides out towards a cosmic explanation and a final theodicy. In consequence it suffers challenge from the rival advance of science. Although religion is a social fact, it is exposed to a purely intellectual refutation. And the defeat of the Church's intellectual claims began the process of secularization, which was to end in the defeat of the Christian community – the final loss of that root experience of membership which shaped European civilization for two millennia and which has caused it to be what it is.

The loss of faith is therefore a loss of comfort, membership and home: it involves exile from the community that formed you, and for which you may always secretly yearn. The great Victorian doubters – Matthew Arnold being pre-eminent among them – were not ready for this experience. They attempted to patch up the social world from purely human resources. And to a great extent they succeeded. Their loss of faith occurred against the background of a still perceivable religious community, whose customs they tried not to disturb. They inhabited the same *Lebenswelt* as the believer, and saw the world as marked out by the institutions and expectations that are the legacy of holiness.

We witness this in the writings of nineteenth-century secularists, such as John Stuart Mill, Jules Michelet and Henry Thoreau. Their vision bears the stamp of a shared religion; the free individual still shines in their world with a more than earthly illumination, and the hidden goal of all their writings is to ennoble the human condition. Such writers did not experience their loss of faith as a loss, since in a very real sense they hadn't lost religion. They had rejected various metaphysical ideas and doctrines, but still inhabited the world that faith had made – the world of secure commitments, of marriages, obsequies and Christenings, of real presences in ordinary lives and exalted visions in art. Their world was a world where the sacred, the forbidden and the sacramental were widely recognized and socially endorsed.

In that brief moment on Dover Beach, Arnold glimpsed the void beneath the moral order that he was constantly patching. And he turned away from it, refusing to mourn the loss of his former certainties. This state of mind found idealized expression in the Gothic Revival, and in the writings of its principal high Victorian advocate, John Ruskin. Nobody knows whether Ruskin was a vestigial Christian believer, a fellow traveller, or an atheist profoundly attached to the medieval vision of a society ordered by faith. His exhortations, however, are phrased in the diction of the King James Bible and the Book of Common Prayer; his response to the science and art of his day is penetrated by the spirit of religious inquisition, and his recommendations to the architect are for the building of the Heavenly Jerusalem. The Gothic style, as he described and commended it, was to recapture the sacred for a secular age. It was to offer visions of sacrifice and consecrated labour, and so to counter the dispiriting products of the industrial machine. It would be, in the midst of the utilitarian madness, a window on to the transcendental, where once again we could pause and wonder, and where our souls would be filled with the light of forgotten worlds. The Gothic Revival – both for Ruskin and for the atheist William Morris, as it had been for the devout Catholic Augustus Pugin – was an attempt to reconsecrate the city as an earthly community built on hallowed ground.

This project, of shoring up the religious worldview by replicating its outward signs, was successful at first. But it depended much on others – on the priests and schoolmistresses who would purvey the old religious teachings, long after the intellectual elite had lost its faith in them; on the families who would bring up their children in the faith, their own doubts notwithstanding; and on the communities who would acknowledge the religious customs and ceremonies, while holding their scepticism at bay. A survey of the English population taken in the mid-nineteenth century, before the composing of 'On Dover Beach', revealed that already, in the cities, 50 per cent of the population had ceased to attend the churches. By the turn of the century the faithful were a minority in England and the reaction was beginning that would eventually chase the symbols of the sacred from the city streets. The last true Gothic cathedral was begun in Liverpool by the 22-year-old Giles (later Sir Giles) Gilbert Scott in 1903.[1] A quarter of a century later, the same architect designed that brief and beautiful symbol of the English city as it staggered on into the modern world –

---

[1] Note, however, that the expansion of Bury St Edmunds Parish Church into a cathedral, begun in 1960, has been carried out in the Gothic style, thanks to a bequest by the architect in charge, while Guildford Cathedral, begun in 1936, imitates the forms of Gothic architecture in council-house brick.

the K2 telephone box, with classical outline (taken from the neo-classical tomb designed for himself by Sir John Soane), Bauhaus fenestration and an air of gentle secular authority, like an old-fashioned English Bobby.

The Gothic Revival was criticized by the early modernists as a form of architectural dishonesty. Not only did its shapes and details pretend to a kind of labour that was not in fact expended on them; their spiritual meaning was also a lie – an attempt to deny the realities of secular society and the utilitarian order. All subsequent attempts to revive either the Gothic or the classical styles, and to build in our city streets according to the ancient archetypes that first created them, have met with the same criticism. On the face of it, however, the criticism is shallow and unconvincing. The same adverse judgement could have been made of Renaissance classicism, of the original Gothic, of Roman vernacular, of the Greek temple itself – all of which originated in an attempt to perpetuate the contours of a successful settlement and a sacred place, through changes that might otherwise unsettle it. The Victorian builders were not pretending to produce something of their own; they were intending to preserve a spiritual legacy. Their work was like that of someone who strives to conserve a fresco, while rebuilding the crumbling wall on which it has been painted. Such a fresco was the European city: a godly place that was to stand forever, but only on condition that someone from time to time took the trouble to patch it up.

Matthew Arnold and John Ruskin devoted their lives to the defence of Christian culture, even though they had lost their faith in the Christian God. And thanks to them and a thousand other fellow travellers, the world of faith endured, long after faith had withdrawn across the 'naked shingles' of Dover Beach. We should perhaps be more amazed than we are that, 200 years after Hume and Kant demolished the claims of Christian theology, we can enter a village church anywhere in Europe and still watch people whose daily lives are conducted under a blazing secular sun, as they nurture their God in the darkness. The Enlightenment has been with us for two or three centuries, but so too has been the resistance to it. There are poets who have responded to the Enlightenment as a kind of light-pollution, from which pockets of darkness must be salvaged in order that we can see the stars. Arnold was one of them, T. S. Eliot another, Rilke a third. Such artists acknowledge loss, but refuse to mourn it, doing what they can to hold things in place while looking to the future.

I am reminded of the deep-seated conservatism that animated my father, in his search for social justice. Architecture, for him, was a symbol of the

worthwhileness of human settlements, of the decencies and continuities of
the labouring people, and of their determination to possess the land. Like me,
Jack Scruton deplored the bleak interruption of needed continuities. He hated
the modernist repudiation of the past that was defacing the weathered fabric
of our town. He shared the sentiments of Ruskin, for whom architecture is an
invitation to the gods to reside among us. There was no sense, to my father,
in the fight for social justice, if the workers were to be rewarded at the end
of it with a functional apartment in a concrete block overlooking screaming
motorways. They were entitled to their share of enchantment, and this could
come to them only if beauty and order were actively conserved.

Seeing things through my father's eyes, it became obvious to me from the
earliest age that traditional architecture was informed by the desire to hold
on to the city as a place where the signs and symbols of eternal order have
been continually reproduced, and where change has been subjected to an
enduring act of consecration. Our civilization set out in search of the Heavenly
Jerusalem, and we still seek it out in the battered centres of our historic towns.
The pilgrimage to Prague or Venice or Florence is a fixture in the Grand Tour
of the modern atheist. But the relentless desire to erase the sacred face persists:
almost every city now has its equivalent of Paris's Centre Pompidou, implanting
a facetious playground among vistas of order and grace. From that centre of
desecration there radiates Le Corbusier's call for total demolition, for a new
start, for a new kind of city – the city of unbelief, in which meanings will be
openly satirized in mirror glass. All across Asia and the Middle East we see the
building of this new kind of city – a city without corners, without shadows,
without secrets. We Europeans resist the disease as best we can, knowing that
the loss of the city will be a loss too far. And we are surely right: for we are
fighting for the home that we love against those who profit from destroying it.

A similar sentiment has governed the evolution of the Anglican Church
since the Reformation, as people have worked to conserve what was built on
the Christian revelation, while allowing faith itself slowly to seep out from the
hidden pores of the structure. The Anglican Church summarized the dilemma
facing English conservatives at the end of the Second World War. Here was
an institution that had been consciously identified with the country during its
hour of need. It was obvious that it should be conserved: why else had we been
fighting? And in conserving it we should also move on – not mourning the old
Coventry Cathedral whose bombed out shell was to stand as a monument to
the dead, but building next to it a new cathedral that would face forward into

the future. The architect chosen was the modernist Basil Spence in preference
to the aging Sir Giles Gilbert Scott. And the modern artists of the day were
roped in as collaborators, to create a cathedral that would express the Christian
message in forms and images appropriate to modern times. The cathedral was
inaugurated with a requiem from Benjamin Britten – a Requiem that would say
farewell to war.

The Anglican Church has been bound up with a culture and a settlement that
demand religious consecration. The result has been the kind of muddle we see
today: a Protestant church whose liturgy declares it to be Catholic; a national
Church with a worldwide congregation; a repository of holy sacraments, which
is regulated by a secular Parliament; an apostolic communion whose authority
descends from St Peter, but whose head is the English monarch. Looked at from
close to, it is all nonsense, fragments left over from forgotten conflicts, about as
coherent as the heap of broken crockery that remains after a lifetime of marital
quarrels.

But it is part of the conservative spirit of the English not to look too closely at
inherited things – to stand back from them, like Matthew Arnold, in the hope
that they can go on without you. Their institutions, the English believe, are best
observed from a distance and through an autumnal haze. Like Parliament, the
monarchy and the common law; like the old universities, the Inns of Court
and the county regiments, the Anglican Church stands in the background of
national life, following inscrutable procedures, and with no explanation other
than its own existence. It is there because it is there. Examine it too closely and
its credentials dissolve. How then can we receive spiritual comforts from an
institution that is so much a thing of this world? How can we believe in the
Church's power to baptize us, to marry us and to bury us, if we see it merely as
a compromise solution to territorial conflicts that ended long ago?

But it is precisely because of this creative muddle that, since the end of the
seventeenth century, when the Puritans at last calmed down and the clergy
signed up to whatever was needed for a quiet life, the Anglican Church has
played its part in leading the English people into the modern world. It has
baptized, married and buried the English with no sense that it was trampling
on their sensitivities or presuming to ask more of them than the minimum
required by decency. And it has avoided the deep metaphysical questions. It
has gradually ceased to enquire whether it has a rightful claim to holiness,
or whether it has been set in judgement on its congregation. Instead, it has
developed a less anxious and interrogatory role, stepping forward on solemn

occasions with words and music and filling the countryside from time to time with the sound of bells. And it has maintained buildings that are now the principal tourist attraction in every village, and the most important landmarks in our towns. Our churches are symbols of a consecrated England that we know from our poets, painters and composers and from brief glimpses caught from time to time through the turmoil of modern life. Our war memorials are built in a style that derives from them, and when we invoke the sacred duties of remembrance it is in words of Laurence Binyon, hewn from the rock of the Anglican liturgy.

The moment of God's presence which the Jews call *shekinah* and which is the topic of Anglican poetry, from George Herbert to T. S. Eliot, no longer has a place in our literature. The experience that we glimpse in the churches that stand in our towns and villages is largely a memory. But it is a resonant memory. We know that these buildings are not simply places in which quarrelsome people took their conflicts to God for a judgement. They are places where people consecrated their lives and acknowledged that love is more important than profit.

George Orwell wrote in 1941 that 'the common people of England are without definite religious belief, and have been so for centuries … And yet they have retained a deep tinge of Christian feeling, while almost forgetting the name of Christ.' This 'tinge of Christian feeling' had a source, and that source is the Anglican Church, whose messages have not been shouted in English ears like the harangues of the Ranters and the Puritans, but filtered through the landscape, through the web of spires, pinnacles and finials that stitched the townscape to the sky, through the hymns, carols and oratorios that rang out in all their assemblies, and through that fragment of the Prayer Book that many people still recite each day, promising to 'forgive them that trespass against us', while never quite sure what the word 'trespass' really means.

The buildings that the Church of England maintains are not just symbols therefore: they are part of our national identity. They define our spiritual condition even in the midst of scepticism and unbelief. They stand in the landscape as a reminder of what we are and what we have been; and even if we look on them with the disenchanted eyes of modern people, we do so only by way of recognizing that, in their own quiet way, they are still enchanted. Hence those who strive to preserve them include many who have lost the habit of Christian worship, and even atheists like my father, who rejected that habit, and yet saw our churches as a part of our 'heritage', like the village streets around them and the landscape in which they are set. Indeed, our churches now rely for their survival more on their beauty than their use: but in doing so, they testify to the profound usefulness of beauty.

This explains, to my mind, why the English have been especially active in the cause of beauty – devoting their associative genius to the conservation of towns, churches, countryside and national monuments since the middle of the nineteenth century. For beauty tells them that they are at home in the world. It is this sense of being at home that stirs the 'tinge of Christian feeling' to which Orwell referred, and the enduring spirit of charity that stems from it. In the appeal to help the victims of the recent tornado in the Philippines, the people of Britain gave more than the people of all the other European countries put together, a small but eloquent reminder of what it is to live in a country whose institutions have been built from below, and whose settlements are understood as 'ours'. It is precisely such people – those who are at home in their world – who can reach out to the homeless and the stranger elsewhere.

Ancestral patterns of ownership and labour speak to us from our landscape – patterns that have been wiped away from the collective farms of Russia, Hungary, the Czech lands and Slovakia. Jack Scruton lamented the vandalizing of our countryside not only for the loss of vegetation and wildlife, but also for the destruction of a human monument, built over centuries by people who imprinted their life in the soil. The need that he felt for the countryside was not a need for fresh air and vegetation only; it was a need for another and older experience of *time* – not the time of the modern conurbation where things constantly accelerate, and the pace is set by busy strangers, but the time of the earth, in which people work at unchanging tasks and the pace is set by the seasons.

Conservation is about beauty; but it is also, for the very same reason, about history and its meaning. Some have a static conception of history, seeing it as the remains of past time, which we conserve as a book in which to read about things that have vanished. The test of the book is its accuracy, and once deemed to be part of our history, objects, landscapes and houses must be conserved as they were, with their authentic surroundings and details, as lessons for the restless visitor. This is the concept of history that you find in the American 'heritage' trails and historic landmarks: meticulously preserved ephemera of brick and timber, standing on concrete between hostile towers of glass.

My father favoured rather a dynamic conception, according to which history is an aspect of the present, a living thing, influencing our projects and also changing under their influence. The past for him was not a book to be read, but a book to be written in. We learn from it, he believed, but only by discovering how to accommodate our actions and lifestyles to its pages. It is valuable to us because it contains people, without whose striving and suffering we ourselves would not exist. These people produced the physical contours of our country; but they also produced its institutions and its laws, and fought to preserve them. On any understanding of the web of social obligation, we owe them a duty of remembrance. We do not merely study the past: we *inherit* it, and inheritance brings with it not only the rights of ownership, but the duties of trusteeship. Things fought for and died for should not be idly squandered. For they are the property of others, who are not yet born.

Conservatism should be seen in that way, as part of a dynamic relation across generations. People grieve at the destruction of what is dear to them, because it damages the pattern of trusteeship, cutting them off from those who went before, and obscuring the obligation to those who come after. The wastelands of exurbia – such as those which spread from Detroit for 50 miles in every direction – are places where past and future generations have been disregarded, places where the voices of the dead and the unborn are no longer heard. They are places of vociferous impermanence, where present generations live without belonging – where there *is* no belonging, since belonging is a relationship in *history*, a relationship that binds both present and absent generations, and which depends upon the perception of a place as home.

This dynamic relation across generations is also what we mean, or ought to mean, by dwelling. At their best, our conservative endeavours are attempts to preserve a common dwelling-place – the place that is ours. And there is a deep connection in the human psyche between space and time. A locality is marked as ours through the time scale of the 'we'. By bearing the imprint of former generations, a corner of the earth pleads for permanence. And in becoming permanent, it becomes a place, a somewhere. True landmarks identify places by testifying to time. And places in the countryside are subsumed by that older, quieter, diurnal time that still moves and breathes in the human psyche. They are spoiled when this old experience of time can no longer be retrieved from them. They cease then to be themselves, cease to be country places, and become part of the ubiquitous nowhere. It is against that result that my father fought: and he fought on behalf of the common people, who were heirs to a beauty that had shone a light into his soul in the time of our country's need.

The Upanishads exhort us to free ourselves from all attachments, to rise to that blissful state in which we can lose nothing because we possess nothing. And flowing from that exhortation is an art and a philosophy that make light of human suffering, and scorn the losses that oppress us in this world. By contrast, Western civilization has dwelt upon loss and made it the principal theme of its art and literature. Scenes of martyrdom and sorrow abound in medieval painting and sculpture; our drama is rooted in tragedy and our lyric poetry takes the loss of love and the vanishing of its object as its principal theme. The greatest epic in English poetry describes the loss of Paradise, and of all the gifts that were there bestowed on us. The questing and self-critical spirit of Western civilization informs both the style of its losses and its way of coping with them. The Western response to loss is not to turn your back on the world. It is to bear each loss *as* a loss. The Christian religion enables us to do this, not because it promises to offset our losses with some compensating gain, but because it sees them as sacrifices. That which is lost is thereby consecrated to something higher than itself.

The loss of religion makes real loss more difficult to bear; hence people begin to flee from loss, to make light of it, or to expel from themselves the feelings that make it inevitable. They do not do this in the way of the Upanishads, which exhort us to an immense spiritual labour, whereby we free ourselves from the weight of Dharma and slowly ascend to the blessed state of Brahma. The path of renunciation presupposes, after all, that there is something to renounce. Renunciation of love is possible only when you have learned to love. This is why, in a society without religion, we see emerging a kind of contagious hardness of heart, an assumption on every side that there is no tragedy, no grief, no mourning, for there is nothing to mourn. There is neither love nor happiness – only fun. In such circumstance, the loss of religion is the loss of loss.

But for conservatives that is not the end of the matter. Western civilization has provided us with another resource, through which our losses can be understood and accepted. This resource is beauty. The features of Western civilization that have made loss such a central feature of our experience have also placed tragedy at the centre of our literature. Our greatest works of art are meditations on loss – every kind of loss, including that of God himself, as in Wagner's *Götterdämmerung*. These works of art do not merely teach us how to cope with loss: they convey in imaginative form the concept that more fortunate people were able to acquire through the elementary forms of the religious life – the concept of the sacred. This is what Nietzsche had in mind, I suspect, when he wrote – shortly before going mad – that 'we have art so that we may not perish of the truth'.[2] The scientist may have seen through to the truth of our condition, but it is only one part of the truth. The rest of the truth – the truth of the moral life – must be recovered in another way.

We recover the truth by re-covering the void. The void that Matthew Arnold perceived beneath the world that he was busy restoring will always be there. But we can cover it by our own devices, not staring into it mournfully until we faint and fall, but turning away from it, and shoring up the structures that it threatens. We should live in the spirit of our Remembrance Sundays, seeing our losses as sacrifices that have purchased the reprieve that we still enjoy. And we should resist those who wished to turn their backs on loss completely, to sweep away the shadows and the corners and the old loved doorways, and to replace the city with a great glass screen above the chasm, into which we will stare forever more.

[2]   The remark is available in the posthumous collection known as *The Will to Power*. See Erich Heller, *The Importance of Nietzsche* (Chicago and London: University of Chicago Press, 1988), Chapter 9.

Index

This index categorizes the principal subject matter of conservatism, culture, law, religion, society and values as general topics, and in more detail by different terms.